NO SEX, PLEASE– WE'RE BRITISH

A Comedy

by Anthony Marriott and Alistair Foot

samuelfrench.co.uk

FOR AMATEUR PRODUCTION ENQUIRIES

UNITED KINGDOM AND WORLD
EXCLUDING NORTH AMERICA
plays@samuelfrench.co.uk
020 7255 4302/01

Each title is subject to availability from Samuel French,
depending upon country of performance.

THINKING ABOUT PERFORMING A SHOW?

There are thousands of plays and musicals available to perform from Samuel French right now, and applying for a licence is easier and more affordable than you might think

From classic plays to brand new musicals, from monologues to epic dramas, there are shows for everyone.

Plays and musicals are protected by copyright law, so if you want to perform them, the first thing you'll need is a licence. This simple process helps support the playwright by ensuring they get paid for their work and means that you'll have the documents you need to stage the show in public.

Not all our shows are available to perform all the time, so it's important to check and apply for a licence before you start rehearsals or commit to doing the show.

LEARN MORE & FIND THOUSANDS OF SHOWS

Browse our full range of plays and musicals, and find out more about how to license a show

www.samuelfrench.co.uk/perform

Talk to the friendly experts in our Licensing team for advice on choosing a show and help with licensing

plays@samuelfrench.co.uk   020 7387 9373

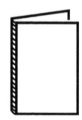

Other plays by ANTHONY MARRIOTT published and licensed by Samuel French

Darling Mr. London

Home is Where Your Clothes Are

No Room For Love

Shut Your Eyes And Think of England

Uproar in the House

Other plays by ANTHONY MARRIOTT published and licensed by Samuel French

Uproar in the House

FIND PERFECT PLAYS TO PERFORM AT
www.samuelfrench.co.uk/perform

MUSIC USE NOTE

Licensees are solely responsible for obtaining formal written permission from copyright owners to use copyrighted music in the performance of this play and are strongly cautioned to do so. If no such permission is obtained by the licensee, then the licensee must use only original music that the licensee owns and controls. Licensees are solely responsible and liable for all music clearances and shall indemnify the copyright owners of the play(s) and their licensing agent, Samuel French, against any costs, expenses, losses and liabilities arising from the use of music by licensees. Please contact the appropriate music licensing authority in your territory for the rights to any incidental music.

IMPORTANT BILLING AND CREDIT REQUIREMENTS

If you have obtained performance rights to this title, please refer to your licensing agreement for important billing and credit requirements.

NO SEX, PLEASE—WE'RE BRITISH

First presented by John Gale for Volcano Productions Ltd, on June 3rd, 1971 at the Strand Theatre, London, with the following cast of characters:

PETER HUNTER	Anthony Valentine
FRANCES HUNTER	Linda Thorson
ELEANOR HUNTER	Evelyn Laye
BRIAN RUNNICLES	Michael Crawford
LESLIE BROMHEAD	Richard Caldicot
SUPERINTENDENT PAUL	Gordon Whiting
MR NEEDHAM	Dennis Ramsden
SUSAN	Janet Mahoney
BARBARA	Vikki Richards
DELIVERY MAN	David Shaw

The play directed by Allan Davis
Setting by Hutchinson Scott

The action passes in a flat over a sub-branch of the National United Bank in a respectable town in the Thames Valley

ACT I
    Scene One   A Monday in June, 9 a.m.
    Scene Two   Early evening, two days later

ACT II   Later the same night

Time – the present

ACT I

Scene One

The curtain rises on an empty set. It is the main living area of a medium-sized flat over a sub-branch of the National United Bank on the outskirts of a respectable town in the Thames Valley. The flat has been nicely modernized and converted from the Georgian original and the overall effect is of warmth and comfort but not opulence. The furniture is all new—mostly modern and in good taste. Down left a door opens off stage into the second bedroom. Up left centre a door gives access to the main bedroom. Next to it—and set back facing the audience—is the front door leading to a passage and then (ostensibly) stairs down to the ground floor. Adjoining the front door is a flight of stairs leading to a small landing and a return. Next to the stairs are the double swing doors to the kitchen. Facing the audience is a dining counter between the main living area and the kitchen. The opening is at present almost completely obscured by an attractive wooden hatch. In front of the kitchen counter there is a fold down table and two chairs. Next to the kitchen hatchway is a door opening into the bathroom and lavatory. The only other remaining door is half-way down right which leads into the study.

The rest of the furniture and fittings include a small desk and chair adjoining, a studio couch with a long stool in front of it; a rocking chair, a trolley set with drinks with a portable television on the lower shelf, and a long occasional table behind the settee. When the hatch is up we can see the interior of a luxury kitchen with two sinks,

*fitted cupboards, electric cooker and so on. On one side
of the main door there is a wall speaker connected to
the bank below. When it is used, the voices on the other
end can be heard quite clearly. On the other side of the
main door there is a telephone which connects to the
speaker downstairs outside the side door of the bank.
Voices will also be heard clearly on this. The telephone
is used for identification and there is a downstairs door
release switch by the side of it. There is no fireplace
in the room. Artificial light is mainly provided, when
required, by wall lights and table lamps.*

*There is a moment's silence and then we hear voices
from behind the hatch.*

PETER *(offstage)* ...Frances, more coffee darling?

FRANCES *(offstage)* I'll do it, Peter. You eat your cornflakes.

PETER *(offstage)* Thanks.

FRANCES *(offstage)* It's all right. Sit still. I can reach over.

PETER *(offstage)* Sure you can manage, dar...? *(He stops in
mid-word. There is a silence)*

FRANCES *(offstage)* Wait a moment—your tiepin—it's caught
on me.

As **FRANCES** *attempts to free* **PETER**'s *tiepin from her
dressing-gown, the counter hatch suddenly shoots up.*
PETER *is a bright and energetic young executive who
is clearly going a long way with the National United
Bank. He has a good sense of humour and is normally
sensible and stable although these qualities are shortly
to be tested to the limit. He is fully dressed in a nicely
cut business suit with white shirt and silk tie.*

FRANCES *is attractive, vivacious and uninhibited. She
is resourceful, amusing and very much a girl of today.
They are a normal, happy, newly married couple—and
enjoying it. They do not have an obsession with sex—for*

its own sake—but they have a warm and healthy relationship and this cannot help but colour the breakfast-time conversation which is otherwise very matter of fact. It is not so much what is said and done but the way it is said and done. FRANCES, *who wears only an attractive dressing-gown, and* PETER *are both sun-tanned.* FRANCES *is distracted for a moment by the hatch.*

What is the matter with that thing? It seems to be taking on a life of its own.

PETER Must be something to do with the counterweights. I'll try and fix it tonight. *(He goes to pour himself another mug of coffee)*

FRANCES Don't move, darling. There's a thread caught on your tiepin. *(She moves in very close to him and frees the clip)*

PETER My God, look at the time. *(He comes out of the kitchen carrying his mug of coffee)* Now have I got my keys with me? Yes. Frances, where did I put my briefcase?

FRANCES Where you left it on Friday night.

PETER Where I left it on... Oh, yes. *(He picks up the briefcase and checks the contents)*

FRANCES *meanwhile comes out of the kitchen with the tiepin.*

FRANCES I can't think why you bother to bring it upstairs at all. I mean you never get round to opening it until Monday morning, do you?

PETER I don't suppose I do—and I can't think why.

The hatch starts to creep down.

(indicating the hatch) Darling.

FRANCES *(pushing the hatch up)* You will see to this thing tonight, won't you, darling?

PETER *(gulping his coffee)* Yes, yes I will.

FRANCES Oh, and the waste disposal needs greasing and that speaker thing— *(Indicates the door intercom)* —needs fixing, I think it's got a loose connection.

PETER Now I know why I never get round to opening my briefcase.

FRANCES So do I... *(Looking at the tiepin)* This tiepin's got an inscription on it. *(Reading) Ex nihilo* what?

PETER *"Ex nihilo, nihilfit."* It's the bank motto: From nothing, nothing comes.

FRANCES It sounds like a permanent credit squeeze. *(As she puts the tiepin on)* Why's Mr Bromhead got a gold tiepin when yours is only silver?

PETER Because he's a district branch manager and I'm only a sub-branch manager, that's why.

FRANCES Well, I think it's ridiculous—having this sort of class distinction in a bank. You haven't had your toast, Peter.

PETER I haven't got time.

FRANCES Yes, you have. I'll get it for you. *(She turns and goes back into the kitchen)*

PETER You haven't forgotten my mother's coming to lunch, have you, darling?

FRANCES No, darling.

PETER Good. Now you know she won't expect anything special— as long as it's all vegetarian. By the way, I don't think it's at all likely—but it is just possible she may want to stay the night.

FRANCES *bangs a cup and saucer on the sink.*

(hesitantly) Are you all right, darling? Did you hear what I said?

FRANCES *(appearing in the kitchen doorway with a plate of toast)* Yes, I heard what you said. You said your mother is staying the night.

PETER No, no, I didn't, darling. What I said was she...she...she might—just might—want to stay the night. I mean I don't think it's in the least likely but it is just possible. She may be too tired to go back to Chelsea.

FRANCES *(firmly and knowingly)* You mean Fulham and you mean she's staying the night.

PETER Well, even if she is, we'll still be on our own. She'll be quite happy upstairs, she told me so.

She just sits and looks at him. He flounders on.

I mean she won't want anything special... I mean she can have the Teasmaid just for one night, can't she?

She still sits and looks at him.

I mean it's not as if she's any trouble and we never use the electric blanket or the radio at night, anyway, and—and—and where are you going, darling?

FRANCES *(turning to the kitchen)* I'm going to get the Kenwood mixer, darling. She might like that as well.

PETER *(injured)* Now there's no need to be like that about it...

FRANCES *(turning back to him)* But we've only been back ten days!

The hatch on the counter shoots down suddenly unaided.

Oh, damn the hatch! You really must fix the wretched thing!

PETER I will, Frances, I definitely will. I'll do it tonight.

FRANCES Then just see that you do.

The bank buzzer sounds loudly.

PETER Hello?

BRIAN 'Morning, Peter. Don't want to intrude on the happy couple...

PETER That's all right, Brian. I was just coming down.

BRIAN *(offstage)* You do know your first appointment's at o-nine-thirty?

PETER I know—Superintendent Paul—about the police sports and social club. Thanks, Brian.

BRIAN *(offstage)* Not at all, not at all. That's what I am here for. Thank you. Good morning.

There is a click and **PETER** *hangs up.*

FRANCES Does that nosey-parker have to be so formal and pedantic every morning.

PETER You know Brian—does everything by the book. If Head Office told him to lose his virginity, he'd do it in triplicate.

FRANCES Actually, I think he's been a bit upset since you were promoted.

PETER Nonsense. He offered to be my best man, didn't he?

FRANCES Offered? Insisted! His toast to the bridesmaids had everything in it but a change in the bank rate.

PETER It wasn't that bad. I've heard worse. I can't remember exactly when but I must have heard worse. Look, I've got to get down to the bank, darling. *(He kisses her)* I'll see you at lunchtime. *(He kisses her again)*

FRANCES Aren't you going to kiss me good-bye?

PETER Yes, of course.

They go into a longer kiss.

(breaking away) Please, darling! I must get downstairs.

As **PETER** *goes to the front door and opens it,* **FRANCES** *goes towards the bathroom and then turns casually.*

FRANCES Give me a buzz if there's any post for me downstairs from London.

PETER *(turning back again)* London? Frances, you haven't started writing off for jobs, have you? Now you promised you wouldn't.

FRANCES *(wide-eyed)* No, no, I haven't been writing off for jobs, darling. I haven't, really I haven't—there was just this advertisement, you see.

PETER What advertisement?

FRANCES In the local paper. Business Opportunities. It was going to be a surprise. And it's only fifty pounds.

PETER Fifty pounds? That's not a surprise. After the cost of this furniture, it's a traumatic shock—Frances, you're not overdrawn, are you?

FRANCES Of course not, darling. I've only sent half of it. The other half's on approval.

PETER Approval? Approval of what?

FRANCES Of the stock, of course. They give you your own area. If I get it, I'll be the only one around here.

PETER Don't tell me. I can see it all now. There's your friendly bank manager in the cupboard and his wife on the doorstep as the Avon lady!

FRANCES No, no, darling. It's the Scandinavian Import Company. Glassware, I think—cutlery, that sort of thing.

PETER Whaat?

FRANCES Anyway, it's very high class. You don't call on people. You have a display and sell it from your own home.

PETER But you can't—you can't run a china shop over a bank! It's their flat. Why do you think Head Office sent poor old Carter from Ealing to Cleethorpes—almost overnight?

FRANCES Did he have an orgy in the strongroom?

PETER No. They found out about his wife's Tupperware parties. What in God's name made you think of such a thing?

FRANCES shakes her head, goes to the studio couch and sits down on it.

FRANCES I wanted to help us, that's all—to get a house of our own with a garden.

PETER But we've only been married three and a half weeks! We're very lucky to get a nice flat like this from the start.

FRANCES I know—but it's not ours. Who wants to live on top of their work with buzzers buzzing all the time?

PETER Oh, darling, you do exaggerate...

The bank buzzer buzzes three times, FRANCES *reacts.* PETER *jumps to the bank intercom and answers it.*

Yes?

BRIAN *(offstage)* Sorry to intrude again but Superintendent Paul's arrived early. He's due in court at o-ten-hundred.

PETER Right, right. I'm just coming down. *(He hangs up and hurries over to* FRANCES*)* Don't worry, darling. We'll get the house and garden without your Scandinavian glass. *(He pulls her up and kisses her)* It was very thoughtful of you, anyway. Forget all about it. I'll see you at lunch. *(He kisses her)* 'Bye.

PETER *exits to the hall.*

FRANCES 'Bye, darling.

FRANCES *goes into the bathroom. Through the open door we hear her running a bath.* FRANCES *comes out of the bathroom. A buzzer sounds by the front door.* FRANCES *hurries and picks up the bank phone.*

Hello? Hello?

FRANCES *realizes it is on the front door not the bank telephone. She hangs the phone up and answers the intercom.*

Hello? Who is it?

ELEANOR *(offstage)* It's me, Frances.

FRANCES Who?

ELEANOR Me, of course, darling, Eleanor.

FRANCES *(astounded)* Eleanor! What? *(Hastily)* I mean what a nice surprise.

ELEANOR *(offstage)* Don't bother to come down, darling. Just release the door.

FRANCES Oh—oh, yes, of course.

FRANCES *switches off the intercom and presses a button by the side of it. She then goes running into the bathroom to switch off the bath. As she goes, she mutters to herself.*

How dare she! How dare she! Half past nine in the morning!

She is now in the bathroom. The water goes off. She reappears and runs across into the main bedroom.

(as she goes) It's a bit bloody much... I've no chance at all now.

FRANCES *is now in the main bedroom. There is a knock at the front door.* FRANCES *comes rushing out of the main bedroom, still dressed only in the dressing-gown.*

I'll tell her—I'll definitely tell her. *(She opens the door all smiles)* Hello, Eleanor. How lovely to see you so early.

ELEANOR HUNTER *enters. She is an extremely elegant, sophisticated woman in her fifties—one who has been well preserved by the West End beauty salons for years. Everything about her is in immaculate taste and expensive. When she is about she likes to do most of the talking—not because she is gushing or feather-brained*

*but simply because she is a very bad listener. To her
snobbery is quite natural. She is carrying a small
overnight valise and a bouquet of flowers.*

ELEANOR Hello, darling. *(She kisses* FRANCES *on the cheek)*
My dear, you look radiant. How nice of you both to invite
me so soon.

FRANCES Not at all.

ELEANOR I thought I might be in the way until Peter said you
were insisting. It really is sweet of you.

FRANCES Not at all.

ELEANOR Of course I wouldn't have been quite so early but
for my driver. My dear, thirty minutes from Chelsea! I'm
sure the man thought he was Graham Hill—but he was
nowhere near as good-looking unfortunately. *(Holding out
the bouquet)* I've bought you a few flowers.

FRANCES How very kind. They're lovely.

ELEANOR *(suddenly noticing* FRANCES' *strange dress)* My dear,
I haven't interrupted you in the middle of anything, have I?

FRANCES No, no—I was thinking of having a bath, that's all.

ELEANOR I always have mine first thing in the morning.

FRANCES So do I usually—I'd better put these in water.

FRANCES *goes into the kitchen carrying the flowers.*

ELEANOR *(looking around her)* So this is the flat I've heard so
much about? My dear, it's charming.

FRANCES *pushes up the kitchen hatch and puts the
flowers in a vase, adding water from the sink.*

Absolutely charming. Hooray for Habitat and Heals! And
it's so much easier to run than a house and garden and
everything. And I'm sure there's masses of room for the
time being.

FRANCES Yes, it's very nice while there are just two of us.

ELEANOR No hurry there, is there, darling? You did promise you wouldn't make me a grandmother until I look at least forty-six. *(Indicating the stairs)* Do those lead to my room?

FRANCES What?

ELEANOR My lovely bedroom Peter was telling me about.

FRANCES Oh, yes, that's right.

ELEANOR Is my bathroom upstairs as well?

FRANCES No— *(Indicating)* —the bathroom's there.

ELEANOR Oh—well never mind. Don't bother about me, darling. I'll just fetch the rest of my things.

ELEANOR exits to the hall.

FRANCES *(to herself)* The rest?

ELEANOR reappears carrying two more smart suitcases— one of which is truly enormous.

Good God—I mean good gracious. Can I give you a hand?

ELEANOR *(going upstairs)* No, thank you, darling. I'll just unpack these for now.

FRANCES Unpack? Oh... *(Light-heartedly)* Well, I must say you seem to have enough there for a fortnight.

ELEANOR *(pausing half-way up the stairs with the two smaller cases in either hand)* My dear, I couldn't possibly impose on you for as long as that. Besides my Health Farm have definitely promised me a room by the end of next week.

ELEANOR sweeps off upstairs.

FRANCES stands there aghast. She just cannot believe what she has heard. Then it dawns; she has heard it. She rushes to the bank phone, and buzzes furiously.

FRANCES Hello, hello.

BRIAN *(offstage)* Good morning, Frances. How are you this morning?

FRANCES I want to speak to Peter.

BRIAN *(offstage)* But he's got Superintendent Paul with him at the moment.

FRANCES I don't care if he's got Pope Paul with him. I want to speak to him now.

PETER *(offstage)* What's the matter, Frances?

FRANCES *(tight-lipped)* Eleanor has arrived with her luggage.

PETER *(offstage)* Oh, yes.

FRANCES I'm surprised she didn't use Pickfords. I think you ought to come up right away.

PETER *(offstage; almost whispering)* But, darling I can't—I've got somebody with me.

FRANCES *(irate)* Yes, and I've got somebody with me—your mother!

ELEANOR *appears on the stairs.*

ELEANOR I just love my room. I'm attached to it already. Peter was so right—it's just the place to spend Christmas.

FRANCES *(staggered)* Christmas?!

ELEANOR And it must be heavenly here in the autumn when the leaves are falling.

FRANCES Yes, I suppose it is. We must take some colour photographs and send them to you.

ELEANOR *(indicating the large suitcase)* I do wish we could get this upstairs. I feel such a mess after the journey.

FRANCES Don't worry. Peter's on his way up now.

ELEANOR He's become so much more considerate since he met you. Thank heaven you two got together before he actually married that dreadful merchant banker's daughter.

FRANCES *(coldly)* Do you mean the one who became a nun?

ELEANOR I shouldn't think so, my dear. She hardly qualified for that one way or the other. But I'm stopping you dressing, aren't I? *(She starts upstairs again)* There's plenty of time to gossip while I'm helping you cook Peter's lunch.

ELEANOR *smiles sweetly and exits.* FRANCES *is possessed. She storms off to the main bedroom. The front door opens and* PETER *comes in. He is carrying a sheaf of papers and cheques.*

PETER *(with his head in the door)* Frances, darling? Brian. Come in, come in.

PETER *comes in and goes to the main bedroom door. He is followed by* BRIAN RUNNICLES *who enters carrying a largish flat cardboard box under his arm.* BRIAN *is about thirty-five, very precise, physically fit and completely devoid of any sense of humour. He does not smoke, he does not drink and girls find him extremely boring company. His life outside the bank is devoted to innumerable honorary activities from Round Table to the local youth club with football refereeing thrown in on Saturdays and Sundays. He is the sort of referee who interprets the laws to the letter and never plays the advantage rule.*

(calling out) You'll never guess, darling. Brian has brought up his wedding present.

FRANCES *enters.*

FRANCES You bloody coward! *(She sweeps past* PETER *ignoring him completely—still dressed in the dressing-gown)* Hello, Brian. You will excuse my casual outfit, won't you? Only somehow it's not been my morning.

BRIAN Oh, dear. I'm sorry to hear that, Frances. I certainly hope I'm going to put that to rights.

BRIAN *gives a humourless little laugh.* **FRANCES** *laughs back artificially.*

As you know, I was hoping to present you both with a rather unusual table lamp—one incorporating a musical bon-bon box, actually. I thought it was rather clever. When you lifted the lid, it played a selection from *The Chocolate Soldier.*

FRANCES How very appropriate.

BRIAN Anyway, when I went back they'd sold it. Still, be that as it may, I thought you might appreciate a little *objet d'art* instead of a little *objet choclat. (He laughs at his own excruciating joke)*

FRANCES *laughs back and turns to* **PETER** *again.*

I do hope you like it. Art is such a personal thing, isn't it?

BRIAN *draws a medium-sized framed reproduction, from the box. It is from an oil still life of a basket of assorted vegetables, a bottle of wine and a large cheese on a check table-cloth.* **FRANCES** *looks at it in disbelief.*

FRANCES Oh... Oh, vegetables. Isn't it nice, Peter? We must hang it in your mother's room while she's with us.

PETER Yes, darling. Er—er—what's it called, Brian?

BRIAN *Légumes Variés de Provence* from an original by Victor Lemauve. It's non-reflecting glass as well. They do a very nice job at Boots.

FRANCES Er, what's that at the bottom, marrow?

BRIAN No, cucumbers actually. The French have very big cucumbers—particularly in Provence. Didn't you notice when you were on your honeymoon?

PETER I can't say we did, no.

BRIAN Oh, yes, they are at least fifty per cent bigger than ours, they force them under glass, you know. Anyway, I'm glad you like it...

PETER *(to* FRANCES*)* Oh, we do, we do, don't we, darling? ...
Well, we'd better get back to the bank, Brian. *(Showing her his fistful of papers)* Just look at this lot. I'm up to my eyes down there.

Before FRANCES *can reply,* ELEANOR *comes hurrying down the stairs.*

ELEANOR Hello, Peter, my darling.

PETER Hello, Eleanor.

ELEANOR How well you look. *(She kisses him on the cheek)* You must be so happy—both of you—as I told Frances before she got dressed—before she was going to get dressed.

PETER Just thought we'd pop up for a minute. You remember Brian Runnicies, don't you?

ELEANOR *(shaking hands)* How do you do? How are you? Weren't you at the wedding?

BRIAN Yes, I was the best man. I made the speech to the bridesmaids if you remember.

ELEANOR *(with edge)* I do indeed. *(Noticing the painting)* Surely that's *Légumes Variés de Provence,* isn't it?

BRIAN *(eagerly)* That's right—from the original by Victor Lemauve.

ELEANOR I know. They shot him in nineteen-forty-four—for collaborating.

BRIAN *(crushed)* Oh, really?

FRANCES Peter, darling, perhaps you'd like to take this up to your mother's room with the rest of her luggage.

PETER Yes, of course, darling. *(He puts down the papers and cheques and goes to pick up the suitcase. He has difficulty in doing so)*

ELEANOR *meanwhile starts up the stairs.*

ELEANOR *(as she goes)* Good-bye, Mr er—er

BRIAN Runniclcs.

ELEANOR —yes. Lovely to have met you again. Tell me, Peter, does that Mr Bromhead often come to this branch?

PETER *(staggering up the stairs)* Of course. He's my senior manager.

ELEANOR *(pausing on the stairs)* I shall look forward to seeing him again. Perhaps I might ask him to dinner...?

PETER *and* ELEANOR *disappear.*

FRANCES *is beside herself again. She just cannot suppress it altogether.*

FRANCES Now we're inviting people to dinner! *(With heavy sarcasm)* Perhaps we should give her a cocktail party while we're about it!

BRIAN *(taking it at face value)* I'm sure she'd like that, Frances. She doesn't seem a bit shy does she?

The front door buzzer sounds.

FRANCES *(tight-lipped)* Oh, good heavens, it's the front door again. Answer it for me. *(She goes towards the main bedroom)* I must get dressed.

FRANCES *goes into the main bedroom.*

BRIAN *answers the front door intercom.*

BRIAN Good morning. Can I help you?

MAN'S VOICE *(offstage)* Postman here, madam. Registered parcel for Mr Hunter.

BRIAN Oh. *(Calling to the bedroom)* Frances—it's the postman. A parcel for Peter. Registered. Shall I fetch it for you?

FRANCES *(offstage)* Would you? Thanks.

BRIAN Not at all. *(To the speaker)* Don't go away, postman. I'm coming right down.

BRIAN *opens the front door and hurries out eagerly. At the same time,* PETER *comes hurrying down the stairs calling back off.*

PETER That's all right, Eleanor. I'll ask Mr Bromhead if he's free for dinner tomorrow.

FRANCES *(offstage)* Whaaat!

PETER Now, Frances.

PETER *exits to the main bedroom.*

FRANCES *(offstage)* If your mother thinks that I am throwing cocktail parties for Mr Bromhead and all her silly friends she's absolutely crazy.

PETER *(offstage)* Don't you worry about Bromhead, darling. I can get us out of that all right.

PETER *enters carrying an electric blanket and transistor in one hand and a Teasmaid in the other.* FRANCES *comes to the doorway, still in her dressing-gown.*

FRANCES I'm sure we're not allowed to run a restaurant over a bank, either.

FRANCES *slams the bedroom door again.* PETER *is becoming very worried. He hurries upstairs.*

PETER *(as he goes)* It's all right, Eleanor, I'll move the wardrobe.

The front door opens and BRIAN *comes in carrying a large brown parcel. He is clearly curious about its contents.*

BRIAN *(calling)* I've got it, Frances. It's quite big. I say, I had to laugh—somebody thinks you're a man. *(He laughs)*

FRANCES *(offstage)* What did you say, Brian?

BRIAN This parcel. It's incorrectly addressed to Mr Frances Hunter. Somebody thinks you're a man, you see. *(He laughs again and turns the parcel over, looking for some clue)*

FRANCES *(offstage)* Sometimes I wish I was.

BRIAN I must say it's jolly well tied up. All the knots are sealed with wax. *(Putting the parcel down)* I'll leave it here. If you'll excuse me, I'd better get back to the bank.

FRANCES *(at the door)* Thanks, Brian. God knows where our scissors are. And we haven't got a sharp knife in the place.

BRIAN *(eagerly)* I've got my old Scout knife with me. Would you like me to do it for you?

FRANCES *(going offstage)* Would you? Thanks.

FRANCES *disappears again.*

BRIAN Not at all, not at all—it's a very professional job. *(He cuts the string on the parcel and removes it)*

FRANCES *(offstage)* Does it say who it's from?

BRIAN No, no, I haven't looked—I mean, well, yes, there is a label on it. Let me see—er—the Scandinavian Import Company.

FRANCES *(offstage) What?* Oh, no!

FRANCES comes running out of the bedroom pulling her shortie dressing-gown on, as she is still only wearing bra and pants.

It's all right, Brian—I'll take it. It's only some wineglasses—I sent for—for the flat—a little surprise for Peter...

She goes to take the box from him and between them they fumble and drop it. The box falls to the floor. To their surprise there is no crash and, instead, a pile of plain envelopes litter the carpet.

BRIAN I'm most terribly sorry. How clumsy of me. Allow me.

FRANCES That's all right—I'll do it. It was my fault.

They both get down on their hands and knees and start picking up the envelopes.

BRIAN Funny sort of glasses, Frances. They feel more like packets of postcards.

FRANCES *(gathering envelopes)* They must have got the orders mixed, the idiots. And they're all sealed down.

BRIAN No, no, this one isn't... *(He starts to withdraw a selection of postcard-sized photographs)* Oh, my God! It's a dirty photo!

FRANCES What are you talking about? Let me see.

BRIAN No, no, I couldn't. You can't possibly look at this— *(Looking at a second card)* —or this. *(Looking at a third card)* And as for this—I'd rather not look myself. *(He surreptitiously slips it into an inside pocket)*

FRANCES *(tearing a packet open)* Don't be ridiculous, Brian. They can't be that bad. *(She looks)* Good lord, they are, too! *(She cannot suppress a laugh)*

BRIAN It's nothing to laugh at, Frances. I'm extremely embarrassed. Peter will be furious if he finds out.

At this moment, PETER appears coming down the stairs. BRIAN and FRANCES are positioned so that he cannot see them and vice versa. The words he overhears stop him in his tracks. As BRIAN blethers on, PETER becomes more and more incredulous.

FRANCES Oh, Brian.

BRIAN It wasn't me—I didn't want to look. You came rushing out, grabbed hold of it and dropped them on the carpet.

FRANCES You admitted you were clumsy.

BRIAN The next thing I knew I was down on the floor looking at a naked girl in a very odd position. Do them up again before Peter comes down.

PETER *(erupting)* Do them up? Do what up?

> **PETER** *notices her partial undress for the first time.*
> *So does* **BRIAN**.

BRIAN Oh, good gracious.

PETER Frances!

BRIAN Frances, look at you... No, no, I'm not looking.

> **BRIAN** *averts his gaze as* **FRANCES** *wraps the dressing-*
> *gown round her.*

PETER Are you interfering with my wife, you randy little chief
cashier?

BRIAN Certainly not. I'm not. She made me cut her string and
hold her little surprise.

PETER *Whaat?!*

BRIAN *(choking)* I tried to keep it from her. I told her it was
pornographic.

PETER Pornographic?

FRANCES Peter, stop it! Stop it at once. It's not his fault at
all—it's all mine.

> **PETER** *turns incredulously.*

PETER What the devil are you talking about?

FRANCES *(picking up the box)* This parcel—from that import
company. They haven't sent glasses at all—it's full of dirty
pictures. Look!

> *She thrusts a sheaf of loose postcards at him.* **PETER**
> *boggles.*

PETER Good god almighty! How can they possibly send stuff
like this through the post? There's three of them here on a
trampoline! It's unbelievable!

> **ELEANOR** *comes down the stairs, looking fresh and crisp.*

ELEANOR It's turning into a gorgeous day. I think it might be quite hot later on. Oh, are those the wedding photographs?

ELEANOR has noticed the prints which PETER is still holding in his hand. He hastily shuffles them together and thrusts them back in the box.

FRANCES No.

ELEANOR No?

FRANCES No, they're Brian's...

BRIAN *(aghast)* Mine?

PETER Yes, mine—er—Minehead. He took them at Minehead—his youth club camp last summer. Thank you very much, Brian. Most interesting. *(He passes the box to BRIAN)*

FRANCES Yes, very interesting, Brian.

BRIAN Yes—I mean, no... *(As PETER passes him the box)* I mean I don't want them.

ELEANOR You don't want them?

PETER No, he doesn't want them looked at—until he's had a chance to touch them up...er, work on them. Here you are, Brian. *(Propelling him to the door)* I expect you want to go back downstairs.

BRIAN Yes... *(Realizing)* I mean no—I mean I don't want to take them downstairs—with the staff and customers—do I?

FRANCES Yes, you do. You said you wanted to take them home at lunch-time.

BRIAN Yes—I mean no—I mean I've just remembered: I'm not going home at lunch-time. It's Round Table Charity Committee, I'm Treasurer, you know. If I leave them here, I can pick them up later, can't I?

A silence.

(plaintively) Can't I?

A silence.

ELEANOR I wish you'd make your minds up. Frances, I don't seem to have a long mirror in my room. Do you have one in yours?

FRANCES Er—yes.

ELEANOR Good. You don't mind if I use it for a minute, do you? Thank you, darling. Good-bye, Mr—er—er...

BRIAN Runnicles.

ELEANOR Yes. You really must show me your camp photographs sometime.

ELEANOR *exits to the main bedroom.*

BRIAN *(quietly seething)* I really do think you owe me an apology, Peter. Look at my badminton club tie. You've pulled my shuttlecock all out of shape.

PETER Never mind that now. We can't leave stuff like this lying around the bank. We've got to get shot of it.

FRANCES It's perfectly easy, darling. We just post it back.

PETER That's just what we can't do: it's a criminal offence. We'd never get it in a letter-box, anyway. We'd have to go to the post office next door.

FRANCES Well, I'm certainly not doing that.

BRIAN No, and I don't blame you either. *(Hastily)* Well, I think I'd better be getting back to the bank, Peter...

PETER Hold on a minute. We've got a very real problem here.

BRIAN I can't see why. You can easily burn them in the garden, can't you?

FRANCES This is a bank flat, Brian. We haven't got a garden.

PETER We haven't got any fireplaces, either. It's all electric.

FRANCES You've got a garden, haven't you, Brian?

BRIAN Yes, I ha—I mean no, no, I haven't got a garden. It's communal—for all the flats—eight flats. I only have twelve and a half per cent—I couldn't do it there. Anyway, it's nothing to do with me.

FRANCES You signed for the parcel, Brian. The Post Office have got your name already.

BRIAN Oh, my God! I'd forgotten that. This is terrible.

PETER Look, we've got to get back to work. *(He takes the box from* BRIAN *and gives it to* FRANCES*)* Here, darling, you'd better hide this somewhere until tonight.

FRANCES Where am I going to hide it?

PETER *(indicating)* Shove it in the wardrobe in the spare bedroom. Nobody ever goes in there.

The main bedroom door opens and ELEANOR *comes out.*

ELEANOR I love your bedroom, darlings. And, of course, that is the spare bedroom, isn't it? You don't mind if I look, do you? I simply must see everything.

ELEANOR *exits to the small bedroom.*

BRIAN *(indicating the study)* What about that room?

PETER The study? There's nowhere to hide it in there.

FRANCES The only cupboard we can lock is in her room. Why don't we put these silly photos straight into the dustbin? They call tomorrow.

PETER We can't do that!

FRANCES Why not?

PETER The dustmen are totting mad round here. It only needs one of them to see these and we're guilty of publishing.

BRIAN *(knowingly)* Quite right. It could be very serious—tantamount to publishing by dustbin.

ELEANOR *enters, hearing the last words.*

ELEANOR What did you say, Mr Runnicles?

BRIAN Oh—er—oo—um...

PETER He was just explaining that—er—er—he has a scant amount of rubbish in his dustbin.

BRIAN Yes, I have a very scant amount of rubbish in my dustbin.

ELEANOR What an extraordinary thing to be talking about at this time of the morning. *(Going to the stairs)* I must go up and finish unpacking. You won't mind if I leave the rest of the flat until later, will you? Thank you.

ELEANOR *exits upstairs.*

BRIAN *suddenly starts laughing inanely.*

PETER What are you laughing at?

BRIAN Well, it's so obvious. I mean it's staring us in the face.

PETER What is?

BRIAN The lavatory.

PETER The lavatory?

BRIAN The lavatory. We tear them up and flush them away.

PETER Don't be ridiculous: that'll take hours.

BRIAN No, it won't. We can do a whole lot at once. Give me some now—I'll have a go. *(He helps himself to a handful of photographs and makes for the bathroom)* I mean I can't just stand around: I've got to do something.

BRIAN *exits to the bathroom.*

FRANCES *(to* PETER, *apologetically)* I'm awfully sorry, darling. I had no idea. Trust me...

The lavatory flushes.

PETER I do, I do. And I'm sorry as well. I should never have gone for Brian like that.

FRANCES *(putting her arms round him)* At least it shows you still care—after three and a half weeks.

PETER *(putting his arms round her)* I do... I do.

Suddenly the bathroom door bursts open and a panic-stricken BRIAN *stands there quivering with fright.*

BRIAN I can't get them down—any of them! They're all floating on top! What are we going to do?

PETER *(breaking from* FRANCES*)* How do I know? It was your idea. Flush it again.

BRIAN It's no use. They keep coming back up. And they look much worse when they're framed.

FRANCES Then for goodness' sake fish them out, Brian. Get something out of the study.

BRIAN *(running to the study)* Oh, this is so ignominious for me. So ignominious!

The bank buzzer sounds on the bank phone. FRANCES *snatches it off.*

FRANCES Hello?

GIRL'S VOICE *(offstage)* Excuse me, Mrs Hunter. Mr Jordon of Jordon Electrics is here to see the manager.

PETER All right, all right. I'll be down in a minute.

FRANCES *(into the phone)* All right, all right. He'll be down in a minute. *(She hangs up)*

The study door opens and BRIAN *hurries out carrying something which, at the moment, we cannot see. He goes straight to the bathroom muttering to himself.*

BRIAN I should never've signed—never've signed. *(He pauses at the bathroom door and turns to* PETER *and* FRANCES*)*

I don't want to seem disloyal, Peter. *(He is pointing with a garden trowel)* But after I've done what I can in here, I sincerely hope I shall then be excused.

BRIAN *exits to the bathroom.*

PETER Frances, we've just got to get rid of these photographs.

FRANCES We'll have to burn them, somehow.

ELEANOR *(offstage)* Peter, darling!

PETER *(going upstairs)* Oh, my God! Look after those. She's probably relaying the carpet by now. Yes, Eleanor, what is it?

PETER *exits upstairs.*

The lavatory flushes again and there is a stifled cry from BRIAN.

BRIAN *(offstage)* Oh, dear me.

FRANCES *looks at the box: she does not know what to do with it. Then she notices a metal waste-paper bin. She places it in the middle of the room, takes four or five photographs out of the box and drops them in the bin. Now she takes a further photograph and sets fire to a corner using a nearby table lighter. The print burns well but when* FRANCES *drops it into the bin, it belches out a cloud of black smoke.* FRANCES *panics and runs about looking for something to put the fire out. She sees a soda syphon standing on the drinks trolley, grabs it and runs back to the bin. Unfortunately, it is empty and when she presses the plunger there is a useless hiss.* FRANCES *panic increases. She dashes to the bathroom, knocks urgently on the door and opens it slightly.*

FRANCES *(in a stage whisper)* Brian—quick—help me!

BRIAN *(offstage)* I can't—I've got my trowel stuck!

FRANCES *runs back to the kitchen counter, seizes the vase containing* ELEANOR's *flowers, rushes to the still smoking bin and, without thinking, tips flowers and water into it. At this precise moment,* ELEANOR's *voice is heard approaching down the stairs.*

ELEANOR *(offstage)* Don't fuss, darling. I shall be quite comfortable eventually.

FRANCES *is now in a blind panic. She notices the box of photographs which she has put down on the sofa. The top is still off. She bangs the top on, grabs the box and looks round wildly for somewhere to hide it. In her excitement the obvious escapes her. She rushes to the rocking chair, puts the box on the seat and then sits down on top of it.*

ELEANOR *comes downstairs to find a still-not-fully-dressed* FRANCES *apparently rocking nonchalantly in the rocking-chair while a waste bin smokes in the middle of the room.* ELEANOR *takes in the scene with some surprise as* PETER *appears.*

(coughing) What have you been doing, my dear?

FRANCES Nothing. Nothing at all. I was burning something—I mean something was burning in the waste bin and I had to put it out. *(In her agitation, she is rocking faster and faster)*

PETER *(hastily)* It must've been Brian. He's terribly careless—leaves a train of cigarette ends wherever he goes.

ELEANOR How extremely dangerous. He ought to be ashamed of himself. *(She notices the stalks sticking out of the bin)* Surely those are not my flowers?

FRANCES Yes—yes, I'm afraid they are. *(She is now rocking like a lunatic)* It was Brian, you see—he panicked—threw them in with the water. But I'm sure they're still all right.

ELEANOR *goes to the waste bin and lifts out a charred and bedraggled flower.*

Oh dear. I'm terribly sorry...

ELEANOR *drops the flower disdainfully back into the bin and looks at her soot-blackened fingers.*

ELEANOR That's all right, dear. It wasn't a special order: Harrod's were delivering, anyway. *(She goes towards the bathroom)* I insist on buying some more, of course.

PETER No, darling. There's really no—where are you going?

ELEANOR *(opening the bathroom door)* My fingers are filthy. *(She turns to go in the bathroom)*

PETER No, no! Could you use the kitchen? ⎱ *(speaking*
FRANCES No, don't! *(She leaps up)* ⎰ *together)*

It is too late. ELEANOR *is already going into the bathroom. She stops abruptly and steps back.*

ELEANOR Mr Runnicles! What do you think you're doing?

BRIAN *appears in the doorway covered in confusion. His jacket sleeves are pulled up and he is holding the trowel in one hand and a wash bag in the other.*

BRIAN Ah—well—er—yes... It's all right, thank you. I've finished now—yes.

ELEANOR But what are you doing in the bathroom with a trowel?

BRIAN Ah—well—er—yes... A trowel in the bathroom? Yes. I took a trowel to the bathroom because—because it's part of a potting set, you see—a garden potting set—for gardeners.

ELEANOR But why have you got it in the bathroom?

PETER Because—because he couldn't find a proper one to do the job, you see. He said he'd do it because he's very good at it, and I'm not, am I, darling?

FRANCES No, hopeless. And it definitely needed doing so he said he'd do it for us because—because he's had a lot of experience of—of...

PETER Of tiling and grouting, haven't you, Brian?

BRIAN I've had a lot of experience...? *(With over-played confidence)* Oh, yes, I've had a lot of experience of trowelling and griting and I was going to do it now. But I don't think I will.

ELEANOR *(giving him an odd look)* I do hope you know what you're talking about—because I certainly don't. *(She goes into the bathroom and looks back at him)* And I do hope, Mr Runnicles, you'll be more careful with your cigarette ends in future.

BRIAN *(blankly)* I beg your pardon?

ELEANOR I'm glad to hear it and I accept your apology. You blackened them all, you know—and they came from Harrods.

The bathroom door closes on **ELEANOR**.

BRIAN *(bewildered)* I've never smoked a cigarette in my life.

PETER Brian, we haven't time to go into that now... We still haven't got rid of these— *(Moving to the desk and opening a drawer)* —but we're going to. There's only one thing to do—and I know what it is. *(He comes back with a large roll of Sellotape)* I've decided to tape it up and dump it as far from here as possible.

BRIAN That's a good idea. That's definitely the best thing to do.

PETER *(to* **FRANCES***)* Tear the label off, darling. Brian'll help you tape it up, won't you, Brian?

BRIAN Yes, yes, I will. *(Taking the Sellotape)*

PETER Good. Just a minute, what's that address! *(Reading)* Scandinavian Import Company. We can't really afford it but I'll make out a cheque.

FRANCES Cheque, darling?

PETER The balance on your—"Swedish glassware". How much was it?

FRANCES and **BRIAN** *are busily taping up the box while* **PETER** *is writing out a cheque.*

FRANCES Twenty-five pounds, I'm afraid darling.

PETER You'd better send them a letter express. Tell them it's all a mistake. *(Tearing off a cheque)* And for God's sake do it right away.

FRANCES Yes, darling. And thank you for being so good about it. *(She kisses* **PETER***)*

PETER That's all right, darling. We'll all be laughing about it this time next week, won't we, Brian?

BRIAN Yes, I expect we will. *(He laughs in his humourless way)* Yes—yes—very droll. Best to see the funny side...

PETER *(ushering* **BRIAN** *and the box to the door)* Yes, well, off you go, Brian. And mind where you dump it.

BRIAN *(still laughing)* Yes, yes, I wi—*whaat!* Me? Dump it? I'm not going to dump it. You said you'd decided.

PETER Yes, I'd decided you were going to dump it. You know Bromhead's coming over today, you're free and I've got Jordan waiting. You've only got to bury it.

BRIAN Bury it!?

FRANCES Yes, you can borrow our trowel again if you want to.

BRIAN I'm sorry, Peter. I really must draw the line. I'd like to help you if I could but I just can't go and do it.

The bathroom door opens suddenly and **ELEANOR** *emerges.*

ELEANOR Peter, there's something very odd about those photographs...

BRIAN Excuse me, I must go and do it.

BRIAN *turns tail and rushes off with the box of photographs and the trowel.*

ELEANOR You'll never believe this, but I think he's been tearing up some of his youth club photographs in there. I found two pieces on the floor. Isn't that part of a trampoline?

PETER Yes. That's why he tore it up—it's out of focus—he was probably jumping up and down when he took it. *(Picking up the papers and cheques)* I must go. I've got a customer waiting. *(To* **FRANCES***)* See you at lunch.

FRANCES Peter—the cheque!

PETER *(handing her the cheque)* Sorry.

PETER *exits.*

FRANCES *folds the cheque without looking at it. She smiles at* ELEANOR.

FRANCES He's getting absent-minded in his old age. *(She drops the label)*

ELEANOR You're getting careless in your old age.

FRANCES *(going to the desk)* You won't mind if I just get this letter done for Peter? *(She sits)*

ELEANOR Of course not. Just pretend I'm not here. You know, Frances. It really is most kind of you to invite Mr Bromhead here to dinner. I do hope he can come. He offered to advise me on my stocks and shares, you know. He thinks my present manager is so lacking in imagination.

FRANCES Is he? Oh, dear.

ELEANOR Of course, it's a problem having capital these days. Quite honestly, darling, if it weren't for you and Peter, I'd go and live in the Bahamas.

FRANCES Oh, damn! *(She starts crossing out furiously)*

ELEANOR But I'm disturbing you, aren't I? I do so want Mr Bromhead to have a high opinion of Peter. I think he's got a great career in front of him. He's always been very good with figures—ever since he was a little boy—just like his father was.

FRANCES There, I've finished.

ELEANOR Have you really, my dear? You have been quick.

FRANCES Yes—I'll just pop next door to the post office.

ELEANOR *(moving to her)* I don't think you can go dressed like that, darling. You'd better let me.

FRANCES But...

ELEANOR Please, darling. I want to buy you some more flowers anyway. You finish dressing. I'll only be a minute.

FRANCES Peter wants it to go express.

ELEANOR All right, darling. I like to make myself useful. I can't bear people who use other people's homes like an hotel! I'd better go and get my handbag.

ELEANOR disappears upstairs.

FRANCES takes a deep breath and restrains herself. She takes the label which was on the box of photos and tears it to shreds. She is going to drop the pieces into the waste-paper basket, then changes her mind. Instead, she goes into the kitchen and puts them down the waste disposal.

ELEANOR enters.

FRANCES You won't forget to express it.

ELEANOR No, I won't. Now I expect you want to finish dressing.

FRANCES Yes, I do.

FRANCES goes into the main bedroom.

There is a knock at the door, which ELEANOR answers.

BRIAN enters carrying the box of photographs.

BRIAN I've made up my mind, I've made up my mind, I've definitely made... Oh!

ELEANOR What do you want?

BRIAN I thought you were Frances.

ELEANOR Frances is getting dressed.

BRIAN Oh. What a pity.

ELEANOR What do you want?

BRIAN Well, Peter asked me to do it for him, but I can't—I can't—see—if you'll excuse me I better be getting back to my position.

BRIAN *exits.*

ELEANOR I dread to think what position that is.

> **ELEANOR** *exits, closing the front door.*
>
> *The bank buzzer sounds.*
>
> **FRANCES** *comes running out of the bedroom, still dressing, and goes to the bank buzzer.*

FRANCES Hello... Who is it?

GIRL'S VOICE *(offstage)* Is the manager there with you, Mrs Hunter?

FRANCES No, he isn't.

GIRL'S VOICE *(offstage)* Oh, dear, he's disappeared and I've got Head Office on.

FRANCES I've got hardly anything on. Good-bye.

> **FRANCES** *exits to the bedroom. There is a pounding offset in the passage and* **PETER** *comes rocketing in the front door, closing it.*

PETER Frances! Darling! Are you there?

> **FRANCES** *enters.*

FRANCES Yes.

PETER You haven't been out yet, have you?

FRANCES No, I've been doing the letter.

PETER What a relief! Where's the cheque?

FRANCES In the letter.

PETER Well, where's the letter?

FRANCES In the post, I expect.

PETER In the post? But you said you haven't been out.

FRANCES I know. Eleanor took it for me. Don't worry I told her to Express it.

PETER Oh, my God, we've had it.

FRANCES Had it? What are you talking about?

PETER That cheque you posted, it was the wrong one. I gave you the wrong one by mistake. Four hundred and fifty.

FRANCES Four hundred and fifty what?

PETER Pounds. We've just sent those sex merchants four hundred and fifty pounds of somebody else's money.

FRANCES How did we do that?

PETER It was the wages cheque from Jordan Electrics and Jordans have just drawn the money!

FRANCES But can't you stop the cheque?

PETER No, I can't, I'd have to tell Mr Bromhead.

FRANCES Mr Bromhead? Why?

PETER Because Jordans have their account at his branch, that's why.

FRANCES Then why are they cashing cheques here?

PETER They have a special arrangement—for their wages. That's why it was a cash cheque. I can't possibly tell Mr Bromhead I've sent their cheque to somebody else, you know what he's like.

FRANCES But this is terrible.

PETER Terrible? It's a disaster. I could lose my job. We've got to get that cheque back. Where did you send it? What's the address? Frances, we're all right—what have you done with the label?

FRANCES I tore it—and I put it down the waste disposal.

PETER The waste disposal! But can't you remember the address?

FRANCES I can't—I can't remember. Your mother was talking all the time, perhaps she noticed.

PETER Mother.

The front door opens and **ELEANOR** *sweeps in brightly carrying a new bunch of flowers with only the stems wrapped.*

ELEANOR Hello, Frances, oh, Peter, I was lucky: there was hardly anyone in the post office, except—Mr Bromhead! *(Turning back)* Do come in, please, Mr Bromhead! *(Giving* **FRANCES** *the flowers)* Here we are, Frances, I hope these last a little longer.

PETER *is rooted to the spot as Leslie* **BROMHEAD** *enters. He is in his mid-fifties, distinguished and smooth.* **BROMHEAD** *is the senior manager in the area and professionally expects the highest standards from his staff. Socially, he has all the graces.*

BROMHEAD Thank you. Good morning, Frances—Peter. Everything all right downstairs?

PETER Oh, yes—er, fine, thank you, Mr Bromhead, yes.

BROMHEAD Good, liking your new home, Frances?

FRANCES *(laying* **ELEANOR**'s *flowers on top of the kitchen counter)* Very much indeed, thank you, Mr Bromhead. Would you like some coffee?

BROMHEAD Thank you. Before you go downstairs, Peter, I want to warn you about Arnold Needham, one of our bank inspectors. Apparently he's just finished up at Twickenham and I've heard you may be next on his list.

PETER *(aghast)* Next on his list? For an inspection, sir?

BROMHEAD Well, I don't think he'll be calling just to cash a cheque, old chap. *(He smiles)* Now I know Needham of old. He's very meticulous, even checks the key register. Still you've nothing to worry about here, have you?

PETER *(looking at the cheque in his hand and hastily stuffing it in his pocket)* Worry here—nothing at all, sir...

BROMHEAD Glad to hear it.

> **PETER** *backs away and in his confusion pushes the front door shut much too hard. The kitchen hatch falls down like a guillotine cutting off all heads of* **ELEANOR**'s *new flowers.* **ELEANOR** *picks up the stalks and holds them in front of her.*

ELEANOR My flowers!

> *Blackout.*

Scene Two

*It is about 6 p.m. two days later. The kitchen light is
on and the hatch is up.* FRANCES *is in the kitchen, but
out of sight.* PETER *is sitting at the desk—with an "A
to Z of London."*

PETER Clegg Street?

FRANCES No.

PETER Clematis Street?

FRANCES No.

PETER Clementhorpe Road.

FRANCES No.

PETER Clement Road.

FRANCES Yes. Might've been.

PETER Yes. Well, was it Clement Road N.W. Ten, S.W. Nineteen
or Beckenham?

FRANCES *comes to the hatch of the kitchen with a plate
of cocktail snacks in either hand. She is now wearing a
neat and simple summer dress.*

FRANCES It's no good, darling, I can't remember. It's been
nothing but that wretched street guide for the past two
days. Everything from Abbess Close to Zoffany Road. Eleven
thousand street names over and over again. Last night you
even fell asleep on me in the middle of Hornsey Rise.

PETER But we've got to find this wretched company! *(Getting
rattled)* We've got to get that cheque back from Scandinavian
Import Company. I still can't understand why they're not
on the phone.

FRANCES You wouldn't say that if you'd seen all the photographs.
Anyway, how can I concentrate when I'm fiddle-faddling
around with these cheese dips and stuffed olives?

PETER Stuffed? What with—pimentos?

FRANCES No, anchovies.

PETER But Eleanor can't eat them! She's a strict vegetarian, you know that.

FRANCES Then she can damn well unstuff 'em herself, I'm not going to. *(She bangs the ice bucket down on the kitchen counter)* Anyway, there's no time now. *(Bringing the drinks trolley over)* She'll be bringing Mr Bromhead back in a minute.

PETER *(sarcastically)* That'll be nice. I haven't seen Bromhead for at least ten minutes. We have Bromhead for dinner last night—Bromhead for bridge—Bromhead in the bank all day—and now Bromhead for cocktails. He'll be handling all her shares before we know where we are. I'm sick to death of it! Yes, Mr Bromhead—no, Mr Bromhead—good-bye, Mr Bromhead. Hello, Mr Bromhead!

As PETER *is reaching the climax of his tirade the front door opens and* BROMHEAD *comes in followed by* ELEANOR. *She is in a smart two-piece outfit and carries an evening newspaper and a bouquet of flowers.*

BROMHEAD Sorry we've been so long.

ELEANOR Yes, we found the florists were still open. *(Indicating the flowers)* What do you think of these, Frances?

FRANCES Thank you, they're—even better than the others.

ELEANOR No, no, darling. You don't understand; Mr Bromhead brought them for *me*, didn't you, Leslie? If you don't mind me saying so, Frances, I think you'd do better here with extremely hardy perennials.

BROMHEAD *(laughing)* Very good, Eleanor. Very amusing. I like that.

PETER *and* FRANCES *exchange a surprised look on this unexpected use of Christian names.*

FRANCES Er, yes. Well, do sit down, Mr Bromhead.

PETER What would you like to drink, Mr Bromhead, your usual?

BROMHEAD Just a small whisky and water, thank you.

ELEANOR (**PETER** *mouthing exactly the same line*) Dubonnet for me on the rocks with a twist of lemon, please, Peter. Do you think we could possibly find a nice vase for these, Frances?

FRANCES (*making for the kitchen*) Yes, of course.

ELEANOR (*following her into the kitchen*) Yes, I thought I'd have them in my room—in place of *Légumes Variés de Provence*—I do find that cucumber rather overpowering in a bedroom.

FRANCES *and* **ELEANOR** *are now in the kitchen and busying themselves with vase, water and flowers at the sink.* **PETER** *brings over* **BROMHEAD**'s *whisky which he has been pouring at the trolley.*

PETER Here we are, Mr Bromhead.

BROMHEAD (*taking the glass*) Thank you, Peter. (*He looks towards the kitchen and then speaks with lowered voice*) I hope you don't mind, but your mother want to discuss her investments with me.

PETER Not at all, sir.

BROMHEAD What a charming woman. And so attractive.

PETER Yes, sir.

BROMHEAD In many ways, you know, she reminds me of my dear late wife.

PETER (*casually*) Really, sir? (*He starts to cross back to drinks, freezes and turns as the realization of the implication hits him*) Er, really, sir?

ELEANOR (*coming to the kitchen side of the counter with a vase of water and flowers*) I didn't tell you, did I, Peter? Leslie's taking me to the theatre tonight.

PETER (*stunned*) Really, Leslie—er, really, sir?

BROMHEAD It's only the local rep, of course. My wife and I used to go a great deal. It'll be nice to take it up again.

FRANCES (*coming out of the kitchen*) What's playing tonight?

BROMHEAD They're trying out a new musical—*Voices from Valhalla*. It's the first night tonight.

ELEANOR (*through the hatch*) I am looking forward to it. I've always been keen on the theatre ever since I saw *The Mousetrap*. When I was at school, of course. (*She has finished arranging the flowers*) There! Aren't they gorgeous?

BROMHEAD I can see you're an expert at flower arrangement as well, Eleanor.

ELEANOR (*looking up at the hatch*) I don't think I'll leave them here...they'll look nicer over here for the time being.

As **ELEANOR** *takes the flowers and puts them on the occasional table by the sofa,* **PETER** *sits in the rocking chair and* **FRANCES** *comes over to* **BROMHEAD** *with a tray of cocktail snacks and a bowl of cheese dip.*

FRANCES Some cheese dip, Mr Bromhead?

BROMHEAD Thank you—it isn't the garlic one, is it?

FRANCES No, it's the celery.

ELEANOR (*sitting on the couch*) I do think Frances is doing awfully well, don't you, Leslie? I could scarcely boil an egg until I took the Cordon Bleu. And, of course, when one has taken the Cordon Bleu, one doesn't want to boil eggs any more, does one?

FRANCES (*thrusting the tray at her*) Olive, Eleanor?

ELEANOR Thank you, darling. (*She takes one*) Oh, dear, they seem to have anchovies in them.

FRANCES (*innocently*) Have they really? I am sorry. Peter must've opened the wrong jar.

PETER, *who has been trying to have a surreptitious look at the "A to Z", looks up startled.*

PETER I beg your pardon?

ELEANOR It's all right, darling. I know you were only trying to be helpful.

BROMHEAD Mind, my dear. You nearly sat on the *Herald.*

ELEANOR The what, dear?

BROMHEAD The *Herald,* our local newspaper.

ELEANOR I quite like your local paper—it's rather quaint. Good gracious! Listen to this. *(Reading)* "Thames Valley Police were today investigating the shock discovery of shoals of pornographic photographs found floating in the river at Cunningham Lock."

PETER *(sitting bolt upright) Whaat?* It can't be true! *(They look at him and he hastily changes the meaning)* I mean it can't be true: they must be making it up...

ELEANOR I don't think they can be making this up. They've got an eyewitness, darling.

FRANCES An eye-witness?

ELEANOR Yes—a water bailiff. And he says he saw this man drop a parcel into the river.

PETER What man?

ELEANOR They refer to him here as the Phantom Pornographer. But they don't know who he is.

PETER *(relaxing a little)* Oh, they don't know who he is?

ELEANOR No. *(Glancing at the paper)* But the police say they'll get him. They've convinced he's a local man and they've made an Identikit picture.

FRANCES Have they, really? *(With false gaiety)* Did you hear that, Peter? They've made an Identikit. *(She laughs)*

BROMHEAD Yes, that face looks somehow familiar.

FRANCES More Bromdip, Mr Cheesehead?

BROMHEAD No, thank you, Frances. Do they say who's in charge of the case, Eleanor?

ELEANOR *(looking at the paper)* Superintendent Vernon Paul.

BROMHEAD Good—sound man. They're obviously taking it very seriously. And so they should.

PETER Quite so, sir.

BROMHEAD Of course we all know this sort of thing is rife in certain parts of London...

PETER *(hastily concealing the "A to Z")* And more's the pity, sir...

BROMHEAD We don't want this sort of filth and corruption down here.

ELEANOR No, not in a nice old town like this.

BROMHEAD But this sort of thing can spread like the plague. I remember when I was manager at Eastbourne I found my chief cashier with some very questionable Indian books. I sacked him on the spot—shot him out like a rocket.

PETER *(gulping)* Did you—did you really, sir?

BROMHEAD Yes, and I've never regretted it. I'd like to get my hands on some of these filth merchants, I'd give 'em stick!

The front door of the flat bursts open and a panic-stricken **BRIAN** *rushes in brandishing a rolled newspaper.*

BRIAN Peter! Frances! Something terrible's... Oo-er—Mr Bromhead!

BRIAN *is completely flummoxed. He knocks over* **ELEANOR**'*s vase of flowers and then hands the paper to* **FRANCES. ELEANOR, FRANCES, BROMHEAD** *and* **PETER** *all jump up.*

I've got my photo, my photo in the paper.

ELEANOR My flowers—again!

ELEANOR *and* **FRANCES** *go to retrieve the flowers. During the ensuing dialogue* **FRANCES** *fetches a cloth to wipe up any surplus water.*

BRIAN Oh, dear, I'm most terribly sorry... Please, let me. *(He gathers up several flowers and in his confusion and trying to hide the newspaper, puts them in the vase upside down)*

ELEANOR That's the wrong way up!

BRIAN Oh, dear, what am I doing?

ELEANOR Idiot! *(She goes into the kitchen)*

BROMHEAD Runnicles. What the dickens do you mean stampeding in here like an escaped bullock.

BRIAN Ah—well—yes—er—beg pardon?

BROMHEAD I said...

PETER *(hastily)* Ah, well, it was all my fault, Mr Bromhead...

BRIAN Yes, it was all his fault, Mr Bromhead...

PETER You see, he's got a key to the side door...

BRIAN *(pathetically)* Key to the side door.

PETER For use in emergencies.

BRIAN In emergencies.

BROMHEAD Emergencies? There isn't an emergency now, is there?

PETER Oh, no, no, no—there isn't an emergency, now, sir.

BRIAN Emergency.

BROMHEAD Then what the hell were you playing at, Runnicles?

BRIAN *(still a pathetic echo)* Playing at, Runnicles?

PETER *(foundering)* Ah, well, he was playing at—er—playing at...

FRANCES *(coming back)* The town hall.

PETER The town hall? Yes, the town hall. He's playing at the town hall next month.

FRANCES He's taken up amateur dramatics, you know.

BROMHEAD Really? In addition to the youth club football refereeing and the Round Table committee. It's a wonder you have time to come to the bank at all, Runnicles.

BRIAN I try my hardest, sir.

BROMHEAD And, anyway, I don't see what amateur dramatics have got to do with your extraordinary method of entry just now.

PETER Ah, well, it is to do with the Method, sir—that's just what it is to do with—the Method school of acting. You're having trouble with your first entrance, aren't you, Brian?

BRIAN Yes, I'm having trouble with my entrance.

FRANCES So he's following Stanislavsky.

BROMHEAD Then I sincerely hope, for all our sakes, you catch up with him before long. (**BRIAN** *starts to go and falls over* **FRANCES** *who is mopping up water behind him.*) And what classical piece is to be blessed with your electrifying Thespian talent?

BRIAN *(blankly)* Beg pardon?

BROMHEAD What play are you doing?

BRIAN Oh—what play am I doing? What play am I doing?

FRANCES *George and Margaret*—he's playing in *George and Margaret.*

BROMHEAD That's Savory, isn't it?

BRIAN I suppose it's a bit *risqué*, yes.

BROMHEAD *Risqué? George and Margaret?* By Gerald Savory?

BRIAN Gerald Savory? Oh, yes—I mean no.

BROMHEAD You don't seem to know much about it do you. What part are you playing?

PETER He's playing the lead, sir.

BRIAN Yes, I'm playing George.

BROMHEAD George? But it's George and Margaret who are coming to dinner?

BRIAN They are? Oh, dear. Perhaps I'd better go. I don't want to be in the way.

BROMHEAD No, no, you damned fool. George and Margaret are coming to dinner in the play but they never come on to the stage. That's the whole point.

FRANCES Ah, but it's different in the amateur version. They do come on—right at the very end. They like to give everyone a chance, you know.

ELEANOR *(sweeping forward with her restored vase of flowers)* I must say I'm fascinated, Mr Runnicles. Presumably you're not calling on us just to rehearse your entrance in *George and Margaret!*

BRIAN Oh, no, no, no—no. As a matter of fact I wanted—er—some advice on—er—a personal—very personal problem, sir.

BROMHEAD Really? *(Putting his arm round* **BRIAN** *in a fatherly manner)* Well, I'm sure we can use another room for a few minutes. Ah yes, the study. Come on in, old chap, and tell me all about it.

BROMHEAD *is starting to steer* **BRIAN** *towards the study, when the latter suddenly realizes what is happening.*

BRIAN No, no, not in there with you, sir. I meant Peter— Mr Hunter. I want my advice from him.

BROMHEAD *(stopping abruptly, but still with his arm round* BRIAN's *shoulder)* With all due respect, I don't see what sort of problem he can handle that I can't.

PETER *(urgently)* Well, it is rather delicate, Mr Bromhead. He thinks he might be suffering from... *(He whispers close to his ear)*

BROMHEAD's *jaw sags. He slowly and tactfully withdraws his arm from* BRIAN's *shoulder.*

BROMHEAD Oh! Oh, dear. That's different then. Perhaps it would be better coming from a younger man.

ELEANOR *(putting flowers on a table)* If nobody else wants your advice, Leslie, perhaps we could spend a minute or two to look at my stocks and shares.

BROMHEAD Yes, of course, my dear.

ELEANOR I've got the list here...

BROMHEAD *(turning to* BRIAN *quietly)* I should get some ointment for that as soon as possible. *(To* ELEANOR*)* After you, my dear.

ELEANOR Sweet of you, Leslie, I can't wait for you to have a peep at my portfolio.

BROMHEAD *and* ELEANOR *exit to the study.*

BRIAN *goggles after them, then turns on* PETER *as the study door closes.*

BRIAN Get some ointment for it? What did you tell him? What am I supposed to be suffering from?

PETER Never mind all that. What about that? *(Holding up* ELEANOR's *paper)* Brian, why did you drop those photographs in the river?

FRANCES Yes, you said you were going to bury them on the Common.

BRIAN *(loudly)* I tried to!

PETER (*glancing at the study*) Shhh!

BRIAN (*quietly*) I tried to—I took them into these bushes to dig a hole and I tripped over them.

PETER (*loudly*) Tripped over what?

FRANCES (*glancing at the study*) Shhhh!

PETER (*quietly*) Tripped over what?

BRIAN This young couple. They were both lying there without any… It was most embarrassing. I mean she hadn't got her—well, neither of them had—it was extremely disconcerting: I didn't know what to say.

FRANCES What did you say?

BRIAN "Good evening." That's all I had time for. Then he kicked me. There must be a terrible bruise there: he'd still got his boots on.

PETER But what in God's name made you dump the box in the river? Why didn't you bury it somewhere else?

BRIAN I couldn't: there were couples lying everywhere. You seem to forget it was early closing day.

FRANCES Early closing? But that was yesterday. You said you'd got rid of them on Monday—right away.

BRIAN (*floundering*) Yes, yes, I know—but I had to think of—consider all the angles…

PETER You dirty beast! You've been sitting at home leering at them.

FRANCES (*poking fun*) Brian! I'm surprised at you!

BRIAN No, no, I didn't—it wasn't like that at all. The box came undone of its own accord—I mean I only did it as a favour and now the papers are on to it…

FRANCES Yes, yes we know.

BRIAN And that's not all. The police will be after me next. They've already made an Identi-whatsit. The next thing I know, they'll be round asking questions.

There is a loud knocking at the front door. All three jump. FRANCES *goes to the front door.*

They're here, they're here.

FRANCES Yes? Who is it?

PAUL *(offstage)* Good evening, Mrs Hunter, Superintendent Paul here.

FRANCES Superintendent Paul.

BRIAN *(panicking wildly)* It's him! It's him! You've got to get me out of here—I'm a wanted man.

PETER For God's sake keep your voice down! There's no point in panicking. We're all in this together.

BRIAN But I don't want to be in it together. I don't want to be in it at all.

FRANCES *(speaking through the door)* Just a minute, please.

BRIAN I told you before: it's nothing to do with me.

PETER All right, all right, all right. Don't say anything. Leave all the talking to me. *(He nods to* FRANCES*)*

BRIAN *hides behind* PETER *stuffing the two papers inside his jacket as* FRANCES *opens the front door. Superintendent Vernon* PAUL *stands framed in the doorway. He is not a physically large man but in his own quiet way he does have a certain presence. He has come up through the force and is now in his early fifties. During his long career he has seen most sorts of crime and his polite and bland exterior does not totally mask a slightly sinister menace and cynicism. Superintendent* PAUL *is not in uniform. His manner throughout is completely relaxed—apart from his eyes which are ever on the move.*

PAUL Good evening, Mrs Hunter. Is your husband in?

FRANCES Er, yes.

PAUL Good. *(Noticing* PETER*)* Oh, good evening. Mr Hunter. *(Coming into the room)* I wouldn't normally bother you like this but you are rather inviting trouble.

PETER Trouble? *(Moving so as to reveal* BRIAN*)*

PAUL *(noticing* BRIAN *hovering in a corner)* Ah, Mr Runnicles. May I ask how long you've been here sir?

BRIAN About four and a half years.

FRANCES Quarter of an hour, that's all.

PAUL Ah, well, I suppose you must be the culprit then.

BRIAN Culprit? No!

PAUL Yes, one of you's left the side door wide open: I could see it across the street.

PETER *(with obvious relief)* Oh, that's all... *(Hastily)* I mean that's always happening and—and it isn't good enough, Brian.

FRANCES No, Peter's told you before: we've got to keep that door closed. This is bank property after all.

PAUL Exactly, my dear. You will be more careful in the future, won't you, Mr Runnicles?

BRIAN Yes, yes, I will—yes. Yes, well—if that's all I think I'll be off. *(He starts edging towards the front door)*

FRANCES Won't you have a drink with us now you're here, Superintendent?

PAUL That's very nice of you, Mrs Hunter. But I don't think I really ought to as I am on duty.

FRANCES Oh, what a pity.

PAUL Still, as I'm not driving perhaps I could just have a small double.

FRANCES Gin or whisky?

PAUL I'd prefer vodka, if you've got it. Doesn't hang on the breath.

The intercom buzzer to the front door sounds.

FRANCES Answer that, will you, Brian?

BRIAN *has no option as* **PETER** *disappears into the kitchen.*

BRIAN *(into the intercom)* What? Oh, yes... Good evening. Can I help you?

MAN'S VOICE *(offstage)* G.P.O. special delivery 'ere. Parcel for Mr Frances Hunter.

BRIAN *(aghast)* What again!

MAN'S VOICE *(offstage)* I beg your pardon.

BRIAN *(crumbling)* Frances—they've sent some more—I mean there's some more that they've sent—that is there's a parcel— downstairs—there's a parcel downstairs with a man.

FRANCES Must be another wedding present! Pop down and sign for it, will you, Brian?

BRIAN Yes, yes... *(Into the intercom)* I'll be right down. *(He clicks off the intercom and realizes)* No, no, no, no, no.

PETER *(coming out of the kitchen with a new bottle of vodka)* Pop down and sign for it, Brian, there's a good chap.

BRIAN Pardon?

FRANCES Pop down and sign for it, Brian.

BRIAN What do you want me to do?

PAUL They want you to sign for a parcel!

BRIAN I haven't got a pencil.

PAUL The postman will have one, they always do.

BRIAN Oh—yes—yes—that's it then, yes. Excuse me, I've got to go and sign for a parcel...

BRIAN *exits to the hall.*

Superintendent **PAUL** *turns to* **PETER** *as he brings over a drink for him.*

PAUL Anything the matter with Mr Runnicles? He seems in a bit of a state tonight.

PETER Yes, well, it's his new girl friend, you see—she's a little cracker—a queen—a beauty queen—and she's having dinner at his flat tonight.

FRANCES *picks up a plate of sandwiches.*

PAUL What's he doing here then?

FRANCES *(putting down the plate of sandwiches)* Bread! He found he'd run out of bread. So he came round here to borrow a loaf and—and—I expect you're pretty busy at the moment, aren't you, Superintendent?

PAUL *(sipping his drink)* No more than usual, Mrs Hunter.

PETER Aren't you? Only we were reading about you in the paper tonight.

PAUL Oh, the pornography case? Well, where there's somebody selling there's somebody buying and that's how we catch them.

FRANCES I suppose that sort of thing could be an accident—you know, inertia selling. People getting things they haven't asked for.

PAUL That's what they always say, Mrs Hunter—when we catch them. But if they're innocent, why don't they come to us in the first place?

PETER *(the light dawning)* Of course! I mean of course that's what they should do. They'd be all right then, wouldn't they?

PAUL Naturally.

PETER Well, in that case...

PAUL A man's always innocent until he's proved guilty. That's why we have a thorough investigation to prove it.

FRANCES What—that he's innocent?

PAUL No, that's he's guilty.

The study door opens and **ELEANOR** *comes out followed by* **BROMHEAD.**

ELEANOR Thank you Leslie.

BROMHEAD You leave your stockbrokers to me, my dear.

ELEANOR I'm so glad you like the look of my industrials.

BROMHEAD *(seeing* **PAUL***)* Hello, Vernon. This is a surprise. *(He laughs)* Not an official call, I hope.

PAUL No— *(With a look at* **PETER***)* —I was just passing so I thought I'd pop in.

BROMHEAD Allow me to introduce Peter's mother, Mrs Eleanor Hunter. *(To* **ELEANOR***)* This is Superintendent Paul, my dear.

ELEANOR How do you do, Superintendent.

PAUL *(turning on his own kind of charm)* How nice to meet you, Mrs Hunter. It's a great pleasure. Are you...

BROMHEAD *(hastily)* Well, I'd better be off. Can I give you a lift, Superintendent?

PAUL Thanks, I'll be glad of it.

BROMHEAD I'll see you at seven-fifteen, my dear.

ELEANOR If you're going to be here at seven-fifteen, Leslie, I'd better get myself ready. *(She picks up her handbag and nearly knocks over the flowers)* Oh, how silly of me. Good-bye—good-bye.

FRANCES Yes, it's six-thirty; you've got less than an hour.

ELEANOR I'll soon throw myself together.

*   **ELEANOR** *sails off up the stairs with her flowers.*

PAUL *(to* **FRANCES***)* Good-bye, Mrs Hunter. Goodbye—er—Peter. Thanks for the dr—hospitality.

PETER Not at all. Most interesting talking to you.

PETER *opens the door and discloses* **BRIAN** *standing nervously outside trying to make out he has not got a parcel behind his back.*

BROMHEAD Not still rehearsing your entrance for *George and Margaret,* are you, Runnicles?

BRIAN No, no, sir—I just went downstairs and now—now I've come up again.

PAUL Mind what you get up to with your little queen tonight.

BRIAN My little queen!

PAUL *(nudging him)* And don't use all the bread tonight, either. You may feel like a couple of slices in the morning.

BROMHEAD That's a good old-fashioned remedy, Runnicles. Better than ointment. Slap a bread poultice on it.

BROMHEAD *and* **PAUL** *go out, closing the door behind them.*

BRIAN Slap a bread poultice on it, my little queen? What're they talking about? And what am I supposed to be suffering from? I insist upon knowing.

PETER Never mind about that now. Let's have a look at that parcel.

BRIAN *(giving it to him)* You're welcome to it. I'm not having anything to do with this one.

PETER *(to* **FRANCES***)* It looks like the same writing. Is it?

FRANCES *(taking the parcel)* Yes, it is: green ink again.

PETER But why've they sent us more photographs. I'm not going to pay... My God, they must've presented the cheque.

FRANCES What—already?

BRIAN Cheque? What cheque?

FRANCES That's more trouble. We haven't told you about it yet.

BRIAN More trouble? I don't want to know.

PETER All right, all right, I'll deal with the cheque. We've got to get rid of this first. I suppose one of us had better dump it again.

BRIAN *(looking at the parcel; horrified)* Are you out of your minds? I'm not going—dropping things in rivers, skulking in shrubberies and getting kicked in the copse—any more.

FRANCES But this parcel is just what we need. Do you remember the first parcel had a label on it—with the address.

BRIAN Yes, yes, what a good idea. Then one of us—I mean you—can take it back and tell them it was all a mistake. That'll get me—get us—out of trouble, I'll open it.

PETER *(giving* **FRANCES** *a quick but warm kiss)* Thank heaven one of us has got some brains round here. You really mustn't panic like this, Brian. I've told you before: you will jump the gun. You've got to keep cool in a crisis—think things out logically step by step and keep absolutely calm.

BRIAN *(the parcel is now unwrapped)* There's no label on it?

PETER *Whaat!* There's got to be a label. } *(speaking*
FRANCES There must be! } *together)*

BRIAN Calm, calm. There's no label on it!

PETER Perhaps there's something inside. *(Looking in the box)* My God, they're blue films! They've sent us blue films now.

FRANCES There's got to be a label! There's got to be—give it to me. *(She opens the box)* There's a bit of paper here—green ink again. *(She opens the paper out and reads)* "Receipt to be following—with grateful thankings."

BRIAN Grateful thankings. Good heavens, they're not even English! *(Taking the paper)* "Balance credited to your account. Enclosed please to find samples of latest high-quality non-flam safety rollers for tits. P.T.O."

PETER For titles P.T.O. *(He turns over the page)*

Good God, look at this lot—

"Ride a Cock Horse Side Saddle,

Two at a Time, Please,

Dick Turpin Rides again and again and again,

Winnie the Poof,

Jack and Jill forgot the Pill."

FRANCES Yes, but the address. Isn't there any address anywhere?

PETER Not a thing. Even this scruffy note isn't signed. We're worse off than ever now. And what's more, they're non-flam safety. We couldn't burn them even if we had a fire place.

FRANCES I've got it—the waste disposal. Put them down the waste disposal.

BRIAN The waste disposal. *(Picking up the parcel and making for the kitchen)* Let's do it right away. Come on, come on!

FRANCES *follows* **BRIAN** *to one of the kitchen sinks.*

PETER You're panicking again, Brian.

BRIAN There's no time like the present. *(He switches on the waste disposal)* Come on, come on...

PETER *(hurrying into the kitchen)* Don't put the reel in as well!

BRIAN Of course I won't. I'll feed it in. There we are—there we are. What did I tell you? It's doing it perfectly—two at a time, please.

Through the open hatch the three of them can be seen huddled over the sink.

FRANCES Don't do it too fast!

BRIAN No, no, no, I know what I'm doing. Leave it to me. My God, it's jammed. *It's jammed.* Switch it off.

There is a general panic inside the kitchen and a crash.

PETER Look out! Look out! You've got film all over the floor.

FRANCES You bloody idiot! You've done it again!

At this exact moment **ELEANOR** *appears descending the stairs. She is in a long and extremely glamorous housecoat carrying the vegetable picture.*

ELEANOR Frances, darling, can I help you with the washing up?

FRANCES Good God, your mother!

BRIAN I can't get it out—I can't get it out! } *(speaking together)*

PETER Now look what you've done!

> **PETER** *leaps from the sink to the kitchen door.*

PETER *(as* **ELEANOR** *comes to the foot of the stairs)* Oh, hello, darling. Is there anything you want?

ELEANOR I do think these vegetables would feel more at home in the kitchen.

> **PETER** *pulls down the hatch on* **BRIAN**'s *hand.*

BRIAN Ow! That hurt my hand.

> **BRIAN** *bangs the films on the table.*

ELEANOR Was that the front door?

FRANCES Stop it, Brian! You're making it worse.

ELEANOR *(moving forward)* Whatever's going on in the kitchen?

PETER It's all right, darling...

The hatch flies up. **PETER** *jumps to it and hauls it down again.*

ELEANOR What's Mr Runnicles doing in there with Frances?

PETER Ah—ah, he's just helping her to wind up—reel up—er clean up in the kitchen. He's had a bit of an accident in there.

ELEANOR What again? I don't know. The man seems to live here practically. *(Quietly)* You mustn't let him foist himself on you like this. He just doesn't know when to leave.

The swing door to the kitchen opens and **BRIAN** *comes rushing out.*

BRIAN I've got it all up and I'm going... *(He sees* **ELEANOR***)* Oh—oh—oh— *(With a nervous laugh)* —good evening.

ELEANOR Are you leaving already? What a pity. Never mind, it's been very nice meeting you again, Mr Runnicles. Good-bye. *(Shakes* **BRIAN***'s hurt hand)*

BRIAN Ah!

FRANCES *(coming to the kitchen door)* What about the parcel, darling?

PETER Oh—Brian's parcel, yes.

BRIAN My parcel?

PETER Yes, your parcel. It'll be quite all right to put it in the strongroom overnight. But I'm afraid I shall have to ask you to take it away in the morning.

BRIAN But—but—but...

PETER No, it's quite all right. I shouldn't give you my key, of course, but as it's an emergency... *(He gives* **BRIAN** *a key and starts propelling him towards the door)* Mind you pop it through the letter-box on your way out.

BRIAN But—but—but...

PETER Good night, old chap.

FRANCES Good night, Brian. Thank you for everything.

ELEANOR Goodbye, Mr Runnicles.

BRIAN Goodbye... *(The front door is closing)*

BRIAN *is shut out.*

ELEANOR You see what I mean, Peter? He didn't want to go even then.

FRANCES I think he just likes company, that's all.

ELEANOR Rather inconsiderate of him. Doesn't he realize you want to be on your own when you're newly married? Can I help you with the washing-up, Frances?

FRANCES *(starting to clear up glasses and put them on the hatchway)* No, please don't bother. Peter will help me.

ELEANOR *(starting upstairs)* Perhaps I ought to get ready for Leslie anyway. One should never keep a man waiting unless one actively dislikes him. *(She is about to exit, when she stops)* You do get on with Mr Bromhead, don't you, Peter?

PETER Yes—yes, of course.

ELEANOR Good—good. I thought you did.

ELEANOR *exits.*

PETER *and* **FRANCES** *turn and look at each other in horror.*

FRANCES You don't suppose—she can't really be thinking of...?

PETER My God, I should hope not. What a terrible prospect, imagine calling Mr Bromhead "Daddy".

There is urgent knocking at the front door and they both jump. **PETER** *opens the door.* **BRIAN** *stands there grinning and without the parcel.*

All right, Brian. What've you done now?

BRIAN *(coming into the room, very pleased with himself)* What have I done? Solved the whole problem that's what I've done. As I always say, you've got to keep cool in a crisis—think things out logically step by step. So I was running down the passage and I thought to myself spot check, I thought, spot check.

FRANCES Spot check?

BRIAN Yes. Suppose a bank inspector comes here for a spot check and finds Dick Turpin riding around the strongroom again and again and again. That's when I noticed the lorry in the window.

PETER Lorry? What window?

BRIAN The window in the side passage. There was this old lorry stopped at the traffic lights—right by the side door. It was full up with junk just like old Steptoe. So do you know what I did? I slipped outside, put the films on the back. *(He laughs)* The lights turned green, the lorry pulled away and it'll probably be half-way to a scrapyard by now.

BRIAN *laughs again. As he does so there is a loud knock on the door.*

FRANCES That's probably the Superintendent.

PETER Did you leave the side door open again, Brian?

BRIAN Supposing they saw me by the lorry! I must get out of here! *(He hides behind the front door)*

PETER You can't—there's somebody at the door. I'll deal with this.

PETER *opens the front door. A B.R.S. Delivery Man stands outside in green overalls. He carries a clipboard with pencil attached.*

DELIVERY MAN Mr Hunter?

PETER Yes?

DELIVERY MAN British Road Services, sir. Delivery for you—two packages.

FRANCES Packages? What of?

DELIVERY MAN I don't know, madam. We don't pack 'em, we only carry 'em. And that's bad enough. You've got to sign here.

PETER scribbles on the clipboard. The **DELIVERY MAN** *produces a sealed envelope.*

I suppose this is your invoice. It come off.

PETER pushes the door against **BRIAN.**

BRIAN Mind my tummy.

The **DELIVERY MAN** *turns and goes out through the front door, calling as he does so.*

DELIVERY MAN Okay, Sam...

FRANCES and **BRIAN** *turn and stare at* **PETER** *as he nervously opens the envelope.* **PETER** *pulls the invoice from the envelope.*

PETER My God, it's them again. They've sent us some more.

FRANCES Filthy photos? ⎫
                ⎬ *(speaking together)*
BRIAN Blue films? ⎭

PETER No, books! Plastic-bound, illustrated in full colour—*A Thousand and One Perversions.* One and a half gross!

The front door swings open to reveal two enormous cartons being pushed in on a trolley. They completely hide the **DELIVERY MAN** *and practically fill the doorway.*

FRANCES, PETER and **BRIAN** *regard the cartons in utter disbelief and sink, as one, onto the sofa.*

At the same moment **ELEANOR** *comes downstairs.*

ELEANOR More wedding presents?

The curtain falls quickly.

ACT II

It is later the same evening. The hatch to the kitchen is down. The room is now lit by the table and wall lamps. It is unoccupied as the Curtain rises, but the television set is apparently on as loud music is coming from it—a standard like "IT'S A LOVELY DAY TODAY", "EVERYTHING'S COMING UP ROSES", or something equally incongruous.

After a moment or two, the front door opens and PETER *comes in furtively. He is in his shirt-sleeves with tie and collar undone. As he moves to the main bedroom,* FRANCES *comes out of it, carrying a pile of large, identical plastic-covered books.* PETER *takes the books from* FRANCES *without a word and goes out through the front door.* FRANCES *is about to go into the main bedroom again when she glances at the television and then the stairs. She crosses over, switches the TV sound right down and then hurries back into the main bedroom.* PETER *comes back through the front door slightly more breathless and again meets* FRANCES *who has re-emerged with another pile of books.*

PETER How many more for goodness' sake?

FRANCES Only about four dozen, darling.

PETER My God, I've been up and down those stairs fourteen times already. I think I'll take the north face of the Eiger next time.

PETER turns and hurries out through the front door. FRANCES goes towards the main bedroom. She is just about to go inside when ELEANOR comes down the stairs.

She is now wearing a striking cocktail dress, and is carrying a cup and saucer.

ELEANOR I did enjoy that cup of tea, darling. Of course, I normally prefer Lap Sang Soo Chong—but I don't suppose one can get it in tea bags.

FRANCES No, I don't suppose one can. I must remember to ask for you the next time I'm in Tesco's.

ELEANOR Thank you, darling. Have you unpacked those boxes of Swedish glassware yet.

FRANCES No.

ELEANOR I'd love to see what they've sent.

FRANCES They aren't here any more—in the flat, I mean. Peter's taken them downstairs. They sent us the wrong order—far too many—they should've gone to a hotel.

ELEANOR Isn't that typical? One never gets what one orders these days. Those boxes were so enormous I thought you must be planning a cocktail party for me. *(She laughs)* You haven't got a spare emery board, have you? One of my nails is an absolute disgrace.

FRANCES *(hurrying to the main bedroom)* Yes, of course. I'll get it for you.

ELEANOR I must've caught it on my wardrobe. One of the handles is very loose, you know.

FRANCES *(emerging from the bedroom and giving her emery boards)* Is it, really? Oh, dear.

ELEANOR Thank you, darling. Perhaps Peter would like to fix it for me while I'm out. *(She moves to the stairs and starts up)* He's always been so good with his hands—ever since he was a little boy. Something to do with all that energy, I suppose...

ELEANOR *exits upstairs.*

The front door opens and **PETER** *comes in, gasping for breath. He is even more disheveled.*

PETER I can't take much more of this. *(Getting his breath back)* If you hadn't sent the wrong cheque, none of this would have happened.

FRANCES I didn't do it deliberately, did I? At least we've got another invoice with their address on it. *(She massages his shoulders)*

PETER *(taking an invoice from his trouser pocket)* Yes, Templeton Road, Hounslow—that sounds just like Clement Road, Beckenham, doesn't it?

FRANCES I did say I wasn't sure. You don't think we made a mistake sending Brian to Hounslow, do you?

PETER Darling, please! I can't be in two places at once and it is only ten minutes up the M4. He only had to take a simple message after all. He can't possibly make a hash of that.

FRANCES You don't want to take a bet on it, do you?

PETER No, I don't. Brain wouldn't win the three-thirty if he started at quarter past two.

FRANCES Shouldn't he be back by now?

PETER Of course he should—and I'm very worried about it. *(Going into the main bedroom)* Darling, I think I'd rather carry the books. They're charging the van by the hour. Come on, give us a hand.

FRANCES follows PETER into the main bedroom. He comes out almost immediately carrying another pile of books and staggers out through the front door. The front door has hardly closed when ELEANOR starts descending the stairs again with the packet of emery boards.

ELEANOR *(calling)* Frances, darling! *(At the bottom of the stairs)* Thank you so much, darling. You've saved my life.

Before FRANCES can reply, the front door bursts open and PETER dashes in, still carrying the books.

PETER *(distraught)* There's a policewoman with a torch by my van. We... *(He stops abruptly)*

ELEANOR What did you say, dear?

PETER *(blustering)* There's a—a policewoman at—at Triorchy called—er—Myfanwy.

ELEANOR What are you talking about, dear?

PETER Well, Frances and I were—um—discussing unusual names, you see.

FRANCES For the future—in case we need one.

PETER And I remembered there's a policewoman at Triorchy called Myfanwy.

ELEANOR *(thoughtfully)* Myfanwy Eleanor—yes, I quite like that. *(She notices the books)* Aren't those the encyclopaedia your father left you?

FRANCES Yes—yes, they are.

ELEANOR *(trying to take one)* Do let me have a look, darling. He wrote an inscription in one of them.

PETER *(snatching them away)* No, no, no, Frances is wrong! Dad's books are in my office. These are reference books—I mean they belong to the bank—downstairs.

ELEANOR *(turning her head on one side and trying to look at the title on the book spines)* A thousand and one what?

PETER *(turning books round so she cannot see)* A thousand and one—er—conversions. It's all to do with decimilization.

ELEANOR Rather you than me, darling. I wouldn't know a prime figure if I saw one. I still don't understand the decimal thing, anyway. *(She starts up the stairs)* I swear it's been colder since we changed to centigrade.

ELEANOR *exits.*

FRANCES What's all this about a policewoman?

PETER There's one down there by the van. What can you expect when it's parked outside a bank?

The intercom buzzer sounds. **PETER** *jumps.* **FRANCES** *takes a deep breath and goes to the speaker.*

Oh, my God!

FRANCES Yes? Who is it? Who is it?

BRIAN *(offstage)* Hello, Frances. Brian here. I've accomplished my mission but I can't get in. The door seems to be locked on automatic.

FRANCES *(pressing the release switch)* All right, Brian. It's free now.

BRIAN *(offstage)* Thank you. I've had a spot of trouble to deal with but it's all A-OK now.

PETER A-OK—locked on automatic! Who the hell does he think he's calling—mission control?

FRANCES I suppose we lose communications while he makes his re-entry.

PETER Hold these a minute, darling.

PETER gives FRANCES the books.

FRANCES I told you we shouldn't have sent him. I know he's made a mess of it. He's nothing but a bag of nerves.

There is a loud knock at the front door. **FRANCES** *jumps and drops the books all over the floor.*

PETER Frances—please!

FRANCES I'm sorry—I'm sorry.

PETER *(opening the front door)* It's Butch Cassidy!

BRIAN enters, disguised with a drooping moustache, a plastic mac and a flat cap.

BRIAN You do know there's a van outside!

PETER Yes, I do know there's a van outside! I've hired it to shift the books. *(He starts picking them up)*

BRIAN Good gracious! Haven't you got rid of them yet?

PETER You've got a damned nerve. It took me an hour to find a van at all and I've been up and down those stairs like a bloody Sherpa.

FRANCES *(also picking up books)* Don't stand around, Brian. Give us some help.

BRIAN I've had a gruelling time as well, Frances—very gruelling indeed.

FRANCES Gruelling? What're you talking about?

PETER Yes, you've been to Hounslow and back—not riding shotgun for Wells Fargo.

BRIAN I'm not talking about the journey, I'm talking about the Scandinavian Import Company. They weren't there.

PETER What do you mean?

FRANCES Weren't there? } *(speaking together)*

BRIAN No, Templeton Road's an accommodation address—you know, a newsagents with a lot of cards in a glass case outside.

PETER But didn't you see anybody?

BRIAN Not at first. His shop was very dark and then I saw him, the owner. He was a very odd sort of man. He kept looking behind him, and talking out of the side of his mouth like that.

FRANCES But what did he say, Brian?

BRIAN He said— *(Reading from a notebook)* —"I am nothing to do with the company but I can give them a message—I can phone a Mr Niko-laides." So I told him straight: I said you were very upset about the books and films because it wasn't what you were after when you answered the advertisement.

PETER *(exasperated)* But what about the cheque? You didn't forget the cheque, did you?

BRIAN Certainly not. I'm not a fool, you know. I said you wanted the cheque back and this Mr Nikolaides had better send somebody down here with it right away.

PETER You did what? Are you out of your mind?

FRANCES We don't want any Swedish Greeks from Hounslow coming here!

BRIAN *(getting flustered)* Well, how was I to know that? I thought it'd be the best thing to...

The door intercom sounds.

Oh, good heavens!

FRANCES *(on the intercom)* Hello? Who is it?

BROMHEAD *(offstage)* Leslie Bromhead.

FRANCES Fine, fine. Do come up, please.

PETER Come on, come on; we've got to hide these...

FRANCES goes to help.

Frances. You call Eleanor.

BRIAN Oh, this is so ignominous! So ignominious!

PETER and BRIAN go into a frantic scramble to pick up the books. At the same time, FRANCES goes running up the stairs calling to ELEANOR.

FRANCES Eleanor, Mr Bromhead's here.

FRANCES exits.

ELEANOR *(offstage)* All right, darling, I'm ready.

PETER *(to BRIAN)* Brian, supposing your man from Hounslow turns up while Eleanor and Bromhead are here. We've got to get them out of the flat as soon as possible.

BRIAN (*running with the books into the main bedroom*) As soon as I've got all of this behind me the happier I will be. I'm staying in here till they've gone—all of them!

As **PETER** *and* **BRIAN** *disappear into the main bedroom, first* **ELEANOR** *and then* **FRANCES** *come down the stairs simultaneously.* **ELEANOR** *is wearing a fur stole.*

ELEANOR I do hope Leslie hasn't got us a box. I think half the fun of going to the theatre is mixing with the general public.

ELEANOR *opens the door to admit* **BROMHEAD.**

BROMHEAD Good evening, Frances. Oh, how charming you look, my dear. I thought you might care for some chocolates. (*He gives her chocolates in a heart-shaped box*)

ELEANOR That's terribly sweet of you, Leslie. Do sit down. I'm sure we've got masses of time.

FRANCES *reacts with alarm.*

FRANCES No, no, I don't think you should—I mean, I don't think you should leave it too long—because of parking at the theatre.

PETER *comes out of the main bedroom.*

Isn't that so, darling?

PETER (*who has not heard* **FRANCES**) Yes, it is, yes. Good evening, sir—yes.

The faint music on the television now gives way to what is apparently a newscast but the voices are only a mumble and we cannot hear what is being said.

BROMHEAD Good evening, Peter. (*Almost to himself*) I didn't realize there was a parking problem at the theatre these days.

PETER Neither did I, sir. I mean they've got an enormous car park now, haven't they?

FRANCES *(trying to make* PETER *understand)* I know, darling, but I've heard there's often a terrific queue to get in—something to do with the new automatic gates.

PETER *(realizing)* Oh, the new automatic gates? Yes, yes, it takes twice as long now.

ELEANOR It was just the same at Ascot last week.

BROMHEAD That's progress for you. Perhaps we ought to be going then, Eleanor?

ELEANOR I'm entirely in your hands, Leslie.

BROMHEAD Yes. *(He coughs)* By the way, Peter, did you know there's a van parked outside?

PETER A van, sir? No, no, I had no idea. Must be something to do with the *boutique* over the road.

BROMHEAD You might keep an eye on it. You never know.

ELEANOR Good night, Frances. Good night, Peter, darling. Don't bother to wait up for us.

BROMHEAD Yes, get a good night's rest, Peter. Arnold Needham might be here tomorrow for his inspection. Just wanted to warn you. Come along, my dear, we don't want to be late for the *Voices of Valhalla*.

PETER *and* FRANCES *look at each other.*

ELEANOR *(as she goes)* I am looking forward to it, Leslie. Peter tells me they put on marvellous productions—and lose an awful lot of that nice Lord Goodman's money.

The front door closes on ELEANOR *and* BROMHEAD. *Immediately, the main bedroom door opens and* BRIAN *sticks his head out.*

BRIAN Have they gone? Is it all clear now?

PETER It's all clear for you, yes. And thanks for your help!

BRIAN *(coming into the room)* There's really no call for sarcasm, Peter. I have backed you both up to the hilt—done everything I can. No-one could possibly say I left you in the lurch. I wonder if it's safe for me to go now?

FRANCES Go? Before we've loaded the rest of the books? Aren't you going to give Peter a hand?

BRIAN *(dithering)* Well, I'd like to—of course I'd like to...

PETER *(hurrying into the main bedroom)* Come on then, come on—before the man from Hounslow gets here.

BRIAN Oh—oh, very well, then. But that's all then—I'm definitely going to my Round Table, I mean if I'm not there they'll cut off my honorarium.

BRIAN *goes rushing after* PETER *into the main bedroom.*

FRANCES *is about to follow when something on the television obviously catches her eye.*

FRANCES Good Lord—it's the High Street.

PETER *(offstage)* What's that, darling?

FRANCES On the television—it's our High Street. *(She hurries to the TV and turns up the sound)*

PETER *enters from the main bedroom to listen.*

TV NEWSCASTER The sudden outbreak of pornography in the Thames Valley—mentioned on our local bulletin yesterday—took a new turn today. Only two days after photographs were found floating in the river, a consignment of indecent films were found on a lorry taking jumble to St Mark's Church bazaar.

PETER Good God Almighty!

BRIAN *emerges from the main bedroom carrying a great pile of books.*

BRIAN What was that? What did he say?

TV NEWSCASTER The nature of the films was not discovered until one of them was shown to members of the Women's Bright Hour who were expecting a religious travelogue.

FRANCES Oh, no!

PETER Good, God Almighty! } *(speaking together)*

BRIAN It can't be true!

TV NEWSCASTER The projectionist—the vicar, the Reverend Owen Hussey—was not available for comment today. He was among those treated for shock by the St John Ambulance Brigade. The films—which were unlabelled—have been handed over to the local police. Several shoppers escaped injury in Windsor today when a runaway brewer's dray...

FRANCES switches off the television. She and PETER turn to BRIAN who stands open-mouthed.

PETER You great Berk!

BRIAN But—but—but—but...

FRANCES *(derisively)* A lorry loaded with junk just like Steptoe!

BRIAN But-but-but-but-but...

PETER Do you realize what you've done? Every policeman in the place will be after us now. Come on, Frances, you'll have to help.

PETER goes rushing into the main bedroom. FRANCES runs after him calling to BRIAN as she goes.

FRANCES How could you do it to us, Brian? How could you do it to us?

BRIAN I beg your pardon... This is outrageous—trying to carry these bloody great tomes—I could do myself an injury.

The door intercom buzzes.

(calling) Peter, there's somebody at the door!

PETER *(offstage)* No, no, darling, I'll take the rest.

The buzzer goes again. **BRIAN** *looks to the main bedroom, then decides he has to answer. He still has to balance the pile of books.*

BRIAN *(on the intercom)* Yes, yes, who is it?

NEEDHAM *(offstage)* Is Mr Hunter there, please?

BRIAN I don't know. Who wants him?

NEEDHAM *(offstage)* He won't know me. It's confidential business. My name's Arnold Needham.

BRIAN Oh! Are you the man from Hounslow?

NEEDHAM *(offstage)* I came through Hounslow, yes—from Twickenham.

BRIAN Ah, it's about the books and things.

NEEDHAM *(offstage)* You could say that. Who's that speaking?

BRIAN I don't know, you don't know me, I don't want to know. You'd better come up. *(He presses the door release switch, then goes running towards the bedroom, calling)* Peter! Peter! It's the man from Hounslow!

PETER *enters with a pile of books.*

PETER What, already? Thank God for that. We can have the whole thing out with them at last. *(He puts the books on the sofa table)*

FRANCES *comes out of the main bedroom also carrying a pile of books.*

FRANCES Did you say the man from Hounslow?

PETER That's right. Now you'd better leave him to me. There's always a chance he may turn nasty—cut up rough. *(To* **BRIAN***)* Put them in there, Brian.

BRIAN I can't, I'm going into the kitchen.

There is a sharp knock at the door. **PETER** *opens it, to reveal* **MR NEEDHAM** *standing outside.*

BRIAN *scuttles into the kitchen with the books, shutting the door behind him.*

NEEDHAM Good evening. Mr Hunter?

PETER That's right, come in, come in.

NEEDHAM I must apologize for calling so late at night.

PETER Not at all. We're only too pleased to see you so soon.

PETER *is a little nonplussed because* **NEEDHAM** *is not what he expected. He is balding and dapper with heavily-framed spectacles. He is soberly dressed in a pinstripe suit off the peg and carries a small overnight suitcase.* **NEEDHAM** *is indeed precise and slightly officious and this trait is borne out by the row of pens in his breast pocket. As we shall discover he is an insomniac and therefore somewhat restless. He has a nervous habit of clearing his throat frequently.*

NEEDHAM *(coming in)* I hope you don't mind me mentioning it, but did you know there's a van outside?

PETER Yes, my wife and I were just loading it up. This is my wife.

FRANCES How do you do?

NEEDHAM How do you do, Mrs Hunter. I do hope I haven't called at an inconvenient time.

FRANCES Oh, no, not at all. We were just waiting for you.

NEEDHAM *(blankly)* Waiting for me? You knew I was coming?

PETER Of course. That's why we were putting all the books in the van.

NEEDHAM Putting them in the van? Whatever for?

FRANCES So you can take them back to Hounslow.

NEEDHAM I don't want to take them to the Hounslow branch. I want to deal with them here in the morning.

PETER We can't wait till tomorrow! There's all this trouble over the vicar and the Women's Bright Hour.

NEEDHAM Women's Bright Hour?

FRANCES Yes, it wasn't so bad with the cards. We just threw them into the river.

NEEDHAM (goggling) You threw the cards into the river? But what about the records?

PETER Records? Thank God, we've never had any.

NEEDHAM Never had any?

FRANCES No, and if they're anything like the books we don't want any, either.

NEEDHAM Mr Hunter, are you seriously telling me you've thrown the cards away, you've never had any records and you don't propose keeping the books?

PETER That's precisely what I'm telling you. And nothing you can say will make me change my mind either.

NEEDHAM But I've never heard anything like it. (Sarcastically) I suppose you don't keep a key register, either?

PETER No, we don't keep a key register... (He gives a take) Did you say key register?

NEEDHAM Naturally. It's normal banking procedure—not confined to the National United.

FRANCES Aren't you the man from the book people?

NEEDHAM Certainly not. I'm Arnold Needham. I've come to start a bank inspection in the morning.

BRIAN (poking his head through the kitchen doors) Oh, blimey O'Reilly!

NEEDHAM What was that? Who said that?

PETER *(flummoxed)* Oh, good heavens! That was—er—that was our...

FRANCES Parrot—our parrot.

PETER Yes, that was our parrot. We have a parrot, Mr Needham, he always swears when he wants something. *(To* FRANCES*)* You'd better give him another cuttlefish, darling.

FRANCES Yes, darling. *(To* NEEDHAM*)* Will you excuse me? *(With false brightness)* He says, "Pieces of Eight", too, you know... *(She goes into the kitchen, closing the door)*

PETER I'm most terribly sorry, Mr Needham. I thought you were somebody else. Somebody who'd—er—come to collect some private books belonging—er—to my chief cashier, Mr Brian Runnicles.

BRIAN *(poking his head through the kitchen doors again)* You swine!

PETER *(lightly)* There he goes again. I suppose he wanted grit, not cuttlefish. Well, Mr Needham, it's very nice of you to call and let us know you're starting tomorrow.

NEEDHAM That wasn't my prime intention. Actually, I came here to find Mr Bromhead.

PETER Mr Bromhead?

NEEDHAM At his housekeeper's suggestion. Not a very helpful woman, I'm afraid. Seemed totally disinterested in everything merely because it was her night off.

PETER Oh, dear. I'm afraid he won't be back for several hours. He's taken my mother to the theatre.

NEEDHAM What an extremely unfortunate combination.

PETER I beg your pardon?

NEEDHAM Of circumstances, I mean. I finished a day early at Twickenham and my hotel room here isn't available until tomorrow. I was hoping Mr Bromhead could put me up. He has been kind enough in the past.

PETER Oh, dear, that is awkward—yes—it is awkward, yes—yes—I don't know what to suggest.

NEEDHAM Well, if it isn't an imposition, I wonder if I could possibly wait here until he returns.

BRIAN *(poking his head through the kitchen doors again)* Oh, hell!

NEEDHAM *(glancing towards the kitchen)* He does swear a lot, doesn't he? Not that I want to intrude, of course.

PETER Well, actually we—that is my wife and I—were thinking of going out ourselves

FRANCES *emerges from the kitchen.*

—weren't we, darling?

FRANCES Yes, we were thinking of going out ourselves, Mr Needham.

NEEDHAM Oh, please don't stay in on my account. I shall be perfectly happy with the television or one of your books—I see you read a lot.

PETER Yes—as I was saying, we were thinking of going out but then we changed our minds and decided to have an early night instead—didn't we, darling?

FRANCES Yes. We decided to have an early night instead, Mr Needham.

NEEDHAM Don't mind me. I shall be perfectly comfortable here. And I have eaten. I am feeling a little tired. I'm afraid I suffer from chronic insomnia and any rest is more than welcome.

PETER Oh, dear. How very unfortunate.

FRANCES We can't possibly let you sit up until the early hours, Mr Needham. And we have got the bed made up in the spare room. You're more than welcome to it.

NEEDHAM That really is extremely kind of you, Mrs Hunter. You're sure I won't be in the way?

PETER Oh, no, no, no, you won't be in the way. It'll be much better if you're in the spare bedroom. *(To* FRANCES*)* Perhaps you'd like to show Mr Needham where everything is, darling?

FRANCES Yes, of course, darling. *(To* NEEDHAM*)* That's the bathroom over there, Mr Needham, and this is your room over here. *(She opens the door of the small bedroom)*

NEEDHAM Thank you, thank you. Most courteous of you. I think I'll turn in right away if you don't mind. I like an early start in the morning. I always say an hour before breakfast is worth three afterwards. *(He nods wisely)*

NEEDHAM *exits to the small bedroom, shutting the door.*

PETER *and* FRANCES *look at each other in despair.*

PETER Oh, God!

FRANCES Oh, darling!

The kitchen door slides back and BRIAN *comes scuttling out.*

BRIAN That's it. That is it. I have never been so humiliated in my life. I suppose I've got psittacosis as well now!

NEEDHAM *enters hesitantly from the small bedroom.*

NEEDHAM Excuse me, I just wanted to—er—the bathroom.

NEEDHAM *smiles politely at* PETER *and* FRANCES, *crosses and goes into the bathroom carrying a sponge bag.*

BRIAN *tries to hide behind his plastic mac.*

BRIAN That's it. That is it. I am leaving—flying away! This instant.

PETER Well, you might take some books down with you!

FRANCES Yes, Brian, I think that's the least you can do!

BRIAN I beg your pardon.

BRIAN *makes his way to the front door. As he gets there, the buzzer goes on the door intercom.*

There's somebody at the door again—somebody at the door!

PETER Well?

BRIAN I won't answer it.

PETER All right, I'll answer it, all this fuss. *(Into the intercom)* Yes? Who is it?

PAUL *(offstage)* Superintendent Paul here, Mr Hunter.

PETER Good evening, Superintendent.

PAUL *(offstage)* I wonder if I could come up for a minute?

PETER Yes, do. I'll release the door. *(He presses the switch)*

FRANCES The books, the books!

BRIAN No, no, I've got to get away from here. *(He starts galloping blindly round the room)* I'm trapped—it's a manhunt—I've got to get away... *(He makes for the bathroom)*

FRANCES *(to* BRIAN*)* No, no, Brian—not the bathroom.

BRIAN Oh, good heavens! What am I doing—what am I doing?

BRIAN *rushes back into the main bedroom followed almost immediately by* PETER *and* FRANCES *with the pile of books. They throw them into the room.*

(offstage) Oh—ow—that hurt!

PETER *and* FRANCES *hastily close the main bedroom door and try to compose themselves.*

The bathroom door opens and NEEDHAM *comes out.*

NEEDHAM Thank you again, Mrs Hunter. Good night—good night.

PETER Good night, Mr Needham. ⎫
                                   ⎬ *(speaking together)*
FRANCES Good night—good night. ⎭

NEEDHAM *goes towards his room. There is a heavy knocking on the front door.* PETER *leaps towards it.*

NEEDHAM Excuse me, is that Mr Bromhead?

PETER No, no, it's just a friend of ours.

NEEDHAM Oh, sorry. Good night, good night.

FRANCES Good night, Mr Needham, good night.

NEEDHAM *withdraws.* PETER *opens the front door. Superintendent* PAUL *stands outside. He is now in his police uniform.*

PETER Good night—I mean, good evening, Superintendent.

PAUL *(coming just inside the door)* 'Evening, Mr Hunter. Sorry to trouble you again but did you know there's a van parked outside?

PETER *(in mock surprise)* A van? Did you say a van?

PAUL Yes, one of my women constables has made a report about it.

FRANCES Oh, that van? Yes, that's to do with Brian—Mr Runnicles.

PETER That's right. He's hired it to—er—move the youth club camping equipment. He—er—keeps it in there. *(Indicating the study)*

PAUL I just thought I'd check as I was passing. *(He moves to go out)* Where is he, by the way?

PETER Who?

PAUL Mr Runnicles.

FRANCES Oh—he's—he's just popped down for a drink to the Queen's Arms.

PAUL Well, I hope he's not having one for the road. You know our bench—very hot on drinking and driving.

PETER Yes, yes, I have heard, yes. I'll make a point of warning him. Good night, Superintendent.

PAUL *(going)* Good night, Mr Hunter. Good night, Mrs Hunter.

FRANCES Good night—good night.

As **PETER** *closes the front door on Superintendent* **PAUL,** *the main bedroom door opens and* **BRIAN** *rushes out demented.*

BRIAN I heard that! I heard that!

FRANCES *(looking at the door to the small bedroom)* Shhh!

BRIAN *(quietly seething)* Now I'm a drunken driver. Well, I'm not standing for it—I'm not standing for it. I've made up my mind—it's no good arguing with me—I'm going to resign my position with the National United Bank! *(A pause)* What about that then?

FRANCES Oh, don't be so bloody pompous! Who cares whether you resign or not? You're the chief cashier in a sub-branch— not the Governor of the Bank of England!

FRANCES *exits to the main bedroom.*

BRIAN That was nice, wasn't it—that was charming after all I've been through. Even Frances has turned against me now.

PETER Oh, come off it, Brian—talking about resigning, I know things are a bit dodgy at the moment, but it's no worse for you than it is for the rest of us.

BRIAN Oh, yes, it is. It most certainly is. You don't have to rush in there— *(Pointing to the main bedroom)* —every time a door opens.

The door of the small bedroom is opening. **BRIAN** *leaps into the main bedroom and slams the door.* **NEEDHAM** *comes out in his pyjamas. He looks at the slamming door with some surprise.*

PETER My wife—she's just the same with car doors.

NEEDHAM Really? So's mine. But then she's a rather heavy-handed lady with everything.

PETER Oh, yes?

NEEDHAM I'm sorry to trouble you again, but I wonder if I could have a glass of water—my sleeping capsules, you know. *(He indicates a bottle of tablets)*

PETER *(moving to him)* Certainly, Mr Needham. Allow me.

NEEDHAM I'd do it myself, of course—but not having a dressing-gown— your good lady, you understand...

PETER *(taking the bottle from him)* That's quite all right. I'll do it. How many, Mr Needham? *(He goes into the kitchen)*

NEEDHAM Oh, only one. You break it into a little water—they're quite efficacious—and quick acting as well... Oh, dear!

The main bedroom door opens and FRANCES *starts to come out.*

Immediately he sees her, NEEDHAM *is embarrassed and withdraws into his own room again.*

FRANCES Peter! Peter! Where are you?

PETER *(coming out of the kitchen)* In the kitchen.

FRANCES What on earth are you doing in there?

PETER Needham needs water for his sleeping capsule. Put one in this glass, will you?

FRANCES But it won't dissolve.

PETER No, no, you break it first. *(She breaks a second capsule)* What on earth are you doing?

FRANCES Making sure, that's all.

PETER But, Frances...

FRANCES Where are you going?

PETER Now it needs more water. He could eat this with a knife and fork.

FRANCES Do be quick, darling. You've got to help me with Brian. He's got that look again—only worse.

As **FRANCES** *disappears into the kitchen, the main bedroom door opens and* **BRIAN** *peers out nervously. He looks first towards the small bedroom, then round the rest of the room. Now he comes out of the bedroom and makes his way furtively to the front door. He has just got his hand on the door knob when there is a loud banging on the door outside.* **BRIAN** *practically jumps in the air. He goes running back into the main bedroom laughing hysterically.*

BRIAN Ahh! The copper's on the knocker—the copper's on the knocker...!

As the main bedroom door slams behind **BRIAN**, **PETER** *and* **FRANCES** *come rushing out of the kitchen.*

PETER What was that? What the hell's going on now?

There is more knocking at the front door.

NEEDHAM's *door opens and he comes out.*

NEEDHAM Excuse me, is that Mr Bromhead? *(Seeing* **FRANCES***)* Oh, I beg your pardon.

FRANCES *(running to the main bedroom)* That's quite all right. Excuse me. I've just got to shut something up in the bedroom.

FRANCES *disappears into the main bedroom and slams the door.*

There is renewed knocking.

NEEDHAM Do you think that's Mr Bromhead?

PETER No, no, far too early. Another of my friends, I expect.

NEEDHAM You do get a lot of callers here, don't you? You haven't forgotten my sleeping draught?

PETER No, no, I'll bring it as soon as I've answered the door.

NEEDHAM Oh, thank you very much.

> **NEEDHAM** *closes his door.* **PETER** *opens the front door. He is astonished to find two girls,* **SUSAN** *and* **BARBARA,** *standing outside. Both are in their twenties, attractive and smartly dressed. Each carries a small valise.*

PETER Good gracious—I mean good evening.

SUSAN Mr Hunter?

PETER That's right, yes.

SUSAN You've got things well organized here, haven't you?

PETER Have I?

SUSAN Wasn't that a police superintendent who let us in?

PETER I suppose it was—yes.

SUSAN You have got things well organized then. Aren't you going to ask us in?

PETER But—but I don't know you. Who are you?

SUSAN *(coming into the room)* I'm Susan and this is Barbara, my sister. *(Moving towards the study)* It's nice here, isn't it? We've never worked over a bank before, have we, Barbara?

BARBARA *(following)* Uh—uh.

PETER Work here? I'm sorry, who are you?

SUSAN Mr Nikolaides sent us, of course. He said you weren't satisfied.

PETER Good God Almighty! You don't mean you're from the Scandi...

NEEDHAM (*offstage*) Mr Hunter!

PETER Look out, please! It's Mr Needham! Get in! Get in!

The door to **NEEDHAM**'*s room is opening and* **NEEDHAM** *can be heard calling.* **PETER** *grabs both girls who are already by the study door and pushes them somewhat violently inside. They are so surprised they disappear without a sound.*

NEEDHAM (*calling*) Mr Hunter... Oh, there you are. Do you think I could possibly have my sleeping draught now? If I have to wait much longer I might nod off. (*He gives a humourless little laugh*)

PETER (*hurrying up to the kitchen counter in a state of great anxiety*) Of course, Mr Needham. Right away, Mr Needham.

NEEDHAM Thank you.

MR NEEDHAM *goes into his room, leaving the door slightly ajar.*

PETER *picks up the sleeping draught and is moving to the small bedroom when* **SUSAN** *puts her head out from the study.*

SUSAN Mr Hunter, what do you want us to do in here?

PETER (*waving her back inside*) Just wait a minute! You'll have to wait a minute.

SUSAN *disappears.* **NEEDHAM** *reappears in his doorway.*

NEEDHAM What did you say, Mr Hunter?

PETER I said I'm sorry you've had to just wait a minute. (*Handing over the glass*) There we are.

NEEDHAM Much obliged to you. I wonder if you could look at my bedside lamp. It doesn't appear to be working...

NEEDHAM *goes back into his room.* PETER *follows him reluctantly, casting anxious glances towards the study door.*

PETER I'll see to it, Mr Needham.

The small bedroom door closes. Now the study door opens and SUSAN *and* BARBARA *come out.* SUSAN *is carrying her valise.*

SUSAN There's nobody here at all now. It's a bit of a funny set-up. He seemed quite odd about us. But then don't they all?

BARBARA *nods and wanders to the television.*

I wish he'd tell us what they want, then we could get ready. I wonder where the bathroom is? *(She opens the bathroom door)* Oh, good. It's here.

SUSAN *goes into the bathroom and closes the door.* BARBARA *goes back into the study and closes the door. Now the main bedroom door opens and* BRIAN *comes out carrying a pile of books. He is followed by* FRANCES *with a smaller pile of books.*

BRIAN It's all right, Frances—I'm quite calm now—quite calm. I'll just put these books in the van and go home.

FRANCES You do that, Brian. You go straight home.

BRIAN Yes, I will, Frances. That's definitely the best thing for me to do—to go straight home, I'll skip my Round Table.

FRANCES Good. Come on then, help me.

BRIAN I'm sorry I got a bit het up—it was all that knocking and buzzing—my head and that parrot.

FRANCES Yes, but it's all over now, Brian. I should go straight home if I were you.

BRIAN Yes, yes, I definitely will: that's what I'm going to do—go straight home. I think I'd better pop to the bathroom first though, if you don't mind.

FRANCES *(heaving a sigh and going into the kitchen)* I'll put some coffee on. *(She disappears in the kitchen)*

BRIAN I'll skip the coffee. I'll go straight home.

> BRIAN *crosses to the bathroom and is about to open the door when* SUSAN *comes out dressed as before, but carrying her valise in one hand and a large rubber club in the other.*

(almost colliding with her) I beg your pardon.

SUSAN It's all right. It's only rubber.

BRIAN *(blankly)* Oh.

> BRIAN *shows no other reaction at all. He just goes straight into the bathroom and closes the door.* SUSAN *meanwhile hurries over and goes into the study. There is a pause: then the bathroom door bursts open. A demented* BRIAN *comes dashing out. He looks round the room wildly but there's no-one in sight.*

BRIAN Frances! Frances! Come quickly! Something terrible's happened.

> *There is a clatter of crockery from the kitchen and* FRANCES *comes rushing out.*

FRANCES For goodness' sake, Brian! What's the matter now? What've you done?

BRIAN *(gulping)* I haven't done anything. I've seen a young lady with a huge rubber cudgel coming out of the bathroom.

FRANCES With a what?

BRIAN A cudgel! A cudgel! A big rubber cudgel! She'd got it in her hand.

FRANCES Don't be ridiculous. You're starting to imagine things now.

FRANCES *picks up her books from the table, opens the front door and goes out, followed by* BRIAN *with his books.*

BRIAN *(still protesting)* But I didn't imagine it, Frances. I saw it as she came out. She said it was rubber, but I didn't realize until I was inside. Then it hit me between the eyes...

The front door closes. BRIAN *and* FRANCES *have gone. The study door opens and* SUSAN *comes out, followed by* BARBARA.

SUSAN *(moving towards the small bedroom door)* How much longer's he going to keep us hanging about? And why doesn't he want that Mr Needham to see us yet? I know, perhaps we're meant to be a surprise...

The small bedroom door opens and PETER *backs out talking to* NEEDHAM *inside.*

PETER It must be the bulb, Mr Needham. I've got a spare in the kitchen. I'll get it. *(He closes the door)*

SUSAN Don't worry: Barbara's got her Polaroid Swinger with her.

PETER *(swinging round in terror)* What're you doing out here over there? *(He starts babbling almost incoherently and he propels them back)* Will you please, please stay in that room until I've got Mr Needham properly organized?

SUSAN Is Mr Needham the only one who wants seeing to tonight?

PETER Yes, thank goodness. Listen. Mr Needham is a very important man—he's got to be properly looked after—get what he wants. And that's not all. He has this trouble at night which is why he asked me to get one for him. But I thought he'd better have two at once—although, of course, he doesn't know he's having two because I haven't told him— that's why you've simply got to stay in there until they start working on him—the tablets, I mean.

There is a knock at the front door.

Quick! Get in! Get in!

PETER *pushes* SUSAN *and* BARBARA *into the study and goes to answer the door.*

The small bedroom door opens slowly and a woozy NEEDHAM *stands there swaying.*

NEEDHAM Excuse me, is that Mr—er—Bromhead?

PETER No, no, that's my—er—my—my wife.

NEEDHAM Oh, sorry.

NEEDHAM*'s door closes.* PETER *opens the front door.* FRANCES *and* BRIAN *come in still carrying their piles of books.*

PETER Good lord, it is my wife. What're you bringing those back for?

FRANCES Because we can't get near the van. There are two policemen down there with a breathalyzer. *(Sniffling)* It's hopeless, Peter, hopeless. We're never going to get rid of them—never. And it's all my fault.

PETER Please don't cry, darling. It's not your fault. We're all to blame—all of us. What're you going to do about it, Brian?

BRIAN *(walking into the main bedroom like a zombie)* I don't know—I don't know—I just don't know...

FRANCES My God, he's going hysterical again.

BRIAN *disappears into the bedroom and, after a pause, gives vent to strangled hysteria.*

Meanwhile, PETER *takes* FRANCES *in his arms—books and all—and tries to comfort her.*

What're we going to do, Peter? What're we going to do?

PETER I don't know, I don't know, I just don't know.

Both go running into the main bedroom. There is more hysterical laughter, a slap and then silence. PETER *comes out and closes the door and starts towards the study.*

NEEDHAM *(offstage)* Mr Hunter. You haven't forgotten my bulb, have you?

PETER No, I haven't forgotten your bulb.

PETER *goes into the kitchen and returns to* NEEDHAM's *door with a bulb. He knocks.*

Mr Needham. Your bulb.

NEEDHAM I say it's rather a big one.

NEEDHAM *closes the door.* PETER *again makes for the study but just as he gets to the door, more hysterical cries from* BRIAN. PETER *rushes to the bedroom. The door closes. Now the study door opens and first* SUSAN *and then* BARBARA *come out.* SUSAN *is carrying her cudgel and is very briefly dressed, in a fur loincloth.* BARBARA *follows dressed only in a tam-o'-shanter, plaid, and sporran. She carries an enormous plastic thistle. The door slams behind them.* NEEDHAM's *door opens and he comes shambling out half-asleep.*

Excuse me. Is that—Mr—Brom—head?

NEEDHAM's *gaze travels from the front door to* SUSAN *and* BARBARA. *He regards them blearily, turns away and shakes his head. Now he turns back and regards them again.*

Must be the capsules—must be.

SUSAN *and* BARBARA *come across to him.*

SUSAN Are you Mr Needham, darling?

NEEDHAM *(closing his eyes)* Yes, I'm Mr Needham—darling. *(He opens his eyes)* You're real! And you're all starkers—in the nuddy.

SUSAN Yes, and you're going to be all starkers in a minute—in the nuddy. We're going to give you a lovely time.

SUSAN *and* **BARBARA** *seize* **NEEDHAM** *by the arms and push him towards his room, starting to take off his pyjama jacket at the same time.*

NEEDHAM No, no, you mustn't! What're you doing? Let go of my jimmy jam-jams. Help! Please! Somebody help me...!

SUSAN *and* **BARBARA** *exit with* **NEEDHAM** *into his room.*

ELEANOR *and* **BROMHEAD** *enter through the front door.*

BROMHEAD I'm terribly sorry, my dear. I really had no idea it was going to be such a disgusting play.

ELEANOR It's quite all right, Leslie. I'm so glad you booked a box. At least we were able to leave early without jostling with the general public. Have you got a cigarette?

BROMHEAD Yes, of course. I must say it was good of you to take it so well.

ELEANOR Not at all. I still don't see how they can call it a virile, contemporary musical when it's full of effeminate Vikings.

BROMHEAD I don't think they were meant to be—er—like that, my dear: just rather unfortunate casting. I must say the first number—all of them prancing naked in the fjord—was enough for me.

ELEANOR And as for those lyrics! Nobody could say I'm not broadminded. But I'm sure they've never uttered words like those in your theatre before.

BROMHEAD I never thought I'd live to see the day when there was that sort of permissiveness in our lovely old theatre.

ELEANOR I'm sure you didn't. I know they call it the permissive society but nobody ever says who gave them permission. And for what? God alone knows, I don't. No wonder our theatres and cinemas have been closing for years. What sort of people want to see such shows when they can enjoy simple, decent pleasures in their own homes?

There is a strangled male cry from BRIAN *in the main bedroom.*

What was that?

BROMHEAD What was what, my dear?

ELEANOR I thought I heard something. Anyway, it was a delightful dinner, Leslie. And the roast duckling was delicious.

BROMHEAD I'm glad you liked it.

ELEANOR You won't mention it to Peter and Frances, will you? They do love to pander to my vegetarian diet—and I'd hate to annoy them. I wonder where they are? They can't have gone to bed already, surely?

BROMHEAD Well, it would hardly be surprising considering...

ELEANOR Quite. Peter's always been one for a good night's sleep. And, of course, he does need it. He's so conscientious as you know. Would you care for a nice brandy?

BROMHEAD Thank you, my dear, that would be most agreeable.

ELEANOR I'll get it. Let me see. Ah, yes, I left it in the kitchen, didn't I? I was showing Frances how to make *crêpes Suzettes* at lunch-time. I always think they're such a useful standby, don't you? *(She goes into the kitchen)*

BROMHEAD *(going towards the bathroom)* Do you mind if I just wash my hands?

ELEANOR Not at all, Leslie, not at all. Do please make yourself completely at home.

BROMHEAD *disappears into the bathroom. The small bedroom door bursts open and* NEEDHAM *runs out, pyjamas flapping.*

NEEDHAM Let go of my jimmy jam-jams.

SUSAN *appears from the room, grabs* NEEDHAM *and pulls him back inside. As the door bangs shut,* ELEANOR *emerges from the kitchen and* BROMHEAD *comes out of the bathroom.*

ELEANOR What did you say, Leslie?

BROMHEAD Nothing, my dear. I was in the bathroom.

ELEANOR Oh. I thought you said something. Your brandy.

BROMHEAD I say, that's a quadruple.

ELEANOR My dear, I know Peter would insist. Do please sit down. He really does admire you tremendously, you know.

BROMHEAD Does he?

ELEANOR He talks about you constantly. I probably shouldn't say this, but I think he tends to regard you as something of a father figure.

BROMHEAD Does he, really, my dear?

ELEANOR Well, it's not altogether surprising, is it? I mean he lost his father when he was only a little boy. And no matter how hard a mother tries she can never be both *un homme et une femme,* if you see what I mean.

BROMHEAD *Je comprends tous, ma chére.*

ELEANOR *(graciously)* Merci.

BROMHEAD And if it isn't presumptuous of me to say so, he is a credit to you. And you, my dear, are most certainly a credit to him. *(He sips his brandy thinking he might perhaps have gone a little too far)*

ELEANOR That's simply sweet of you, Leslie. *(She leans across and kisses him on the cheek)*

He is so taken aback, he chokes on his brandy.

Oh, dear, I'm so sorry. I've made you spill your brandy.

BROMHEAD *(coughing)* Don't apologize—please—it's only on my tie.

ELEANOR *(jumping up)* I know: there's some spot remover in the spare bedroom. I'll get it for you. *(She is already putting out her hand to the door handle)*

BROMHEAD No, no, please don't bother. It's practically evaporated already.

ELEANOR *(pausing at the door)* Are you sure? I can quite easily...

BROMHEAD No, positive. *(Patting the couch)* Do come and sit down again. I haven't enjoyed an evening like this for years.

ELEANOR Neither have I.

ELEANOR and BROMHEAD reach for their drinks and cross arms in doing so. They laugh and toast each other with "Skol."

And it seems to have gone so quickly.

There is a male cry and a shriek of female laughter from the small bedroom. ELEANOR and BROMHEAD exchange glances.

Good gracious, I'm glad I didn't go in there. What on earth are Peter and Frances doing in the spare bedroom?

BROMHEAD *(roguishly)* Change of scene is as good as a rest, I suppose.

ELEANOR Somehow I don't think that comes into it. I know, perhaps it would be better if we went up to my room, Leslie.

BROMHEAD *(with enthusiasm)* Yes, yes, I think it would.

ELEANOR Bring your brandy. We can have a little chat about Peter—and things. *(She goes to the stairs)*

BROMHEAD *(following)* Oh.

ELEANOR I'm so glad the children didn't come to the theatre tonight. Peter has no time at all for anything in the least bit smutty...

ELEANOR *and* **BROMHEAD** *disappear upstairs. The door to the main bedroom opens slowly and* **BRIAN** *comes out, followed by* **PETER** *and* **FRANCES.**

BRIAN It's no use, Peter, I can't stay on the run like this. I'm going to give myself up—go to the police—confess everything.

PETER Don't talk such utter rubbish, Brian. Anyone would think you were wanted by Interpol.

BRIAN Interpol? Now we're back to that swearing bloody parrot again! Well, I'm at the end of my tether and I've got a pounding headache. I just don't want to argue any more.

FRANCES We can't leave you with a bad head, Brian. You'd better have two of our Disprin.

PETER Disprin. Darling?

FRANCES *(picking up* **NEEDHAM**'s *bottle of tablets from the kitchen counter)* Yes, I wouldn't offer them, darling, if he didn't "need 'em". *(She disappears into the kitchen for a glass of water)*

PETER Need 'em? Oh, yes—yes—he does need them—definitely—I can see that. Good idea, darling.

BRIAN No, no, I don't think I should. They upset my tummy sometimes and I had prunes for lunch, anyway.

FRANCES *(coming back with a glass of dissolved tablets)* These won't upset you, Brian. *(Giving him the glass)* You'll feel a lot better when you've had these.

PETER Two, darling?

FRANCES Two, darling.

BRIAN I'll just have a little sip then.

PETER That's right, Brian. *(Clapping him on the back)* You have a little sip.

BRIAN *(spluttering)* There! Now look what you've made me do. I've swallowed it all.

PETER Have you, really? Oh, dear. Never mind; it can only do good. You come and lie down for a minute or two.

FRANCES Yes, then you'll feel better.

BRIAN Well, just for a minute or two—only a minute or two. Then I want to get out of here...

All three go into the main bedroom. The door closes. The door of the small bedroom is yanked back, there is a whack, and NEEDHAM *comes stumbling out with* SUSAN *and* BARBARA *in pursuit. He is now in his pyjama trousers only and is clutching to hold them up.* SUSAN *carries the pyjama cord and the cudgel, which she is brandishing.* BARBARA *is waving the thistle.* NEEDHAM *is very much under the influence of his sleeping draught and really does not know what he is saying or doing.*

NEEDHAM I can't stand any more. Ladies. Ladies. No sex, please—we're British!

NEEDHAM *staggers into the study. The two girls go in after him and the door closes. There is hardly a pause before* ELEANOR *comes down the stairs.*

ELEANOR I won't be a minute, Leslie. I'll just put the coffee on and get a few biscuits, shall I? I know there's some shortbread.

ELEANOR *goes into the kitchen and emerges, almost at once, carrying a biscuit tin. She is about to remount the stairs when there is a male shout and a lot of female laughter from the study.* ELEANOR *turns, looks at the small bedroom and sees that the door is half open. She looks back to the study, and there is more female laughter. She shakes her head and shrugs.*

What are they doing? Playing musical chairs?

ELEANOR *goes upstairs. The moment she disappears, the door of the study opens again and* **NEEDHAM** *staggers out on the run holding the plastic thistle which is now bent. He goes round the studio couch with* **SUSAN** *and* **BARBARA** *in pursuit.*

NEEDHAM No, no, ladies, please—I don't want to be The Cock of the North. I want to go to beddy-bye-byes.

NEEDHAM *cowers up against the back wall near the bathroom.* **SUSAN** *and* **BARBARA** *approach him stealthily.*

SUSAN Come along, naughty, naughty, Needham!

NEEDHAM *(turning and facing the wall in desperation)* No, no, leave me alone!

SUSAN Get his pyjamas off Barbara.

The main bedroom door opens and **PETER** *backs out. He turns and sees* **SUSAN** *and* **BARBARA** *with* **NEEDHAM**. *He is transfixed for a moment and cannot speak at all. Then he takes a deep breath and rushes across the room waving his arms.*

PETER What in God's name do you think you're doing dressed—undressed—like that? Let go of Mr Needham at once! I'm terribly sorry. It's all a mistake, Mr Needham.

NEEDHAM Mistake, Mr Needham. *(His head drops forward)*

SUSAN Do you mean he doesn't want it?

PETER Of course he doesn't want it—and he shouldn't be getting it. I'm most dreadfully sorry, Mr Needham. It isn't at all what it seems. You see, Mr Runnicles went to Hounslow and...

There is a gentle snore from **NEEDHAM**.

Mr Needham! Mr Needham!

SUSAN He's gone to sleep on us. How insulting.

PETER *(turning on them)* Will you two get out of here? I can't cope any longer. It's got nothing to do with Mr Needham.

SUSAN Why the hell are we here then?

PETER Because of Mr Runnicles. He was the one who sent the message. *(Indicating* NEEDHAM*)* Where's his pyjama cord?

SUSAN *(indicating the study)* In there.

PETER *(hurrying across and going in the study)* This is a disaster—an absolute disaster. Supposing Eleanor came back. And what would Mr Bromhead say?

PETER *exits to the study.*

SUSAN *(to* BARBARA, *following him)* Why didn't he tell us before? It's Runnicles who wants us—Mr Runnicles.

SUSAN *and* BARBARA *disappear into the study, almost closing the door.* FRANCES *comes out of the main bedroom.*

FRANCES It's all right, darling. I've got him lying down.

FRANCES *stops when she realizes the room is apparently empty. She turns and moves towards the kitchen. Now she sees* NEEDHAM *standing up against the wall with head bowed and hands in front of him.*

Mr Needham! What're you doing against the wall? Mr Needham!

PETER *comes out of the study looking very harassed and carrying the pyjama cord. He closes the door behind him.*

(hissing) What's he doing, Peter?

PETER *(crossing to her)* Sleeping.

FRANCES Sleeping?

During the ensuing dialogue, NEEDHAM's *pyjama trousers slowly begin to fall. Neither* PETER *nor* FRANCES *notices until the critical moment.*

PETER I can't explain now. We must get him back to his room.

FRANCES But how did he get there?

PETER Well, it's these girls they've sent from Hounslow.

FRANCES Girls from Hounslow?

PETER Yes, yes, with the sporran and the bludgeon. I've been trying to tell you for ages. Brian's hashed it all up again. They haven't sent us a man for the books, they've sent us two girls for God knows what...

FRANCES *(suddenly noticing* NEEDHAM*)* Peter—his trousers!

PETER Don't look, darling. It's not a pretty sight. *(He leaps to* NEEDHAM, *grabs the falling pyjama trousers and ties them up with the cord)* Mr Needham, pull yourself together.

NEEDHAM *(stirring)* What—what's the matter? What're you doing with my—tassle?

PETER It's all right, Mr Needham. You've had a nasty dream. We're taking you back to bed.

NEEDHAM Thank you. *(His head nods again)*

PETER *takes* NEEDHAM's *right arm round his own shoulder.* FRANCES *takes* NEEDHAM's *left arm round her shoulder.*

FRANCES Come along, Mr Needham. We'll soon have you settled down again.

PETER *and* FRANCES *start to move across the back of the room. They have just reached the front door alcove when* BROMHEAD's *voice rings out from the stairs.*

BROMHEAD *(offstage)* What a splendid idea, Eleanor.

ELEANOR *(offstage)* I'm glad you like my idea, Leslie. I'm sure we'll both enjoy it.

PETER *(aghast)* Good God Almighty! They're back!

FRANCES Leave her to me.

> FRANCES *slips out from under* NEEDHAM's *left arm and rushes half-way up the stairs.*
>
> ELEANOR *appears on the half-landing.*
>
> PETER *meanwhile staggers under* NEEDHAM's *weight and tries desperately to keep him out of* ELEANOR's *eye-line.*

(with terrible false brightness) Hello, Eleanor. You're back early.

ELEANOR Hello, Frances. Still dressed? We were sure you'd gone to bed. Where's Peter?

FRANCES *(with a vague gesture)* Oh, he's around—around and about.

ELEANOR The theatre was very disappointing. Still I'm sure you've enjoyed a quiet evening on your own. I was just going to pour the coffee.

> PETER *is still staggering around with* NEEDHAM. *He realizes he is getting nowhere and the danger is becoming more acute. In desperation he steers* NEEDHAM *to the front door and props him up against the right-hand wall.*

FRANCES There's no need. I'll do it. Peter and I were going to have some, anyway.

ELEANOR Oh, good. We can all come down and have it together.

PETER *(dashing to the foot of the stairs)* No, no, no, don't do that. Hello, darling. We'll come up there and have it with you... *(He is practically pushing* ELEANOR *upstairs)*

ELEANOR There's no need to push me, Peter!

FRANCES I'll fix the coffee and come up as quick as I can.

PETER *pushes* ELEANOR *off upstairs.*

PETER Thank you, darling.

FRANCES *rushes dementedly to the kitchen counter, pushes the hatch up and starts pouring coffee into one cup. She pours the second cup of coffee and then takes the bottle of sleeping tablets. She puts one into the first cup and is about to replace the top when she has second thoughts. To make sure, she puts a tablet into the other cup. She is about to pick up the tray when* NEEDHAM *groans.* FRANCES *goes to the front door alcove, and finds* NEEDHAM *starting to slide down the wall towards the floor.*

FRANCES Mr Needham! (*She grabs hold of him and is trying to haul him upright when* PETER's *voice is heard*)

PETER (*off; desperately*) Frances! Coffee, darling! Please!

FRANCES Coming—coming... (*Pushing* NEEDHAM *back against the wall*) Just stay there, Mr Needham. I'll see you again.

FRANCES *runs to the kitchen counter, picks up the tray and cups and makes her way upstairs as quickly as she can.*

NEEDHAM (*meanwhile*) Yes—see you again. (*Sings dopily and sadly*) "I'll see you again, Whenever spring breaks through again..." Dah, dah, dah, dah, dah, dah... (*He snores*)

The main bedroom door opens and BRIAN *staggers out. He is in shirtsleeves and waistcoat and his collar and tie are undone.* BRIAN *is in the same comatose state as* NEEDHAM *and clearly does not know where he is or what he is doing. He feels his way along the wall to the front door where he stands facing* NEEDHAM *with his eyes closed.*

(*stirring*) "I'll see you again..."

BRIAN *(with eyes closed)* "Whenever spring breaks through again..."

BOTH *(in harmony)* Dah, dah, dah, dah, dah, dah, dee...

BRIAN *(opening his eyes)* Who sang that?

NEEDHAM Sir Noël Coward.

BRIAN Pleased to meet you, Sir Noel. I want to confess everything—I want to do it now.

PETER *comes hurrying down the stairs two at a time.*

PETER But you must have a second cup, I'll bring the percolator up. *(He arrives at the front door alcove and finds* NEEDHAM *and* BRIAN *face to face)* Good God, they're forming a guard of honour now! *(He grabs* BRIAN *first, picks him up and puts him on the sofa stool)* What the hell do you think you're doing, Brian?

BRIAN I want to do it now—I want to confess...

PETER Sit there a minute: don't go away... *(Now going to* NEEDHAM*)* Come along, Mr Needham... *(He slaps his face several times)* Wake up, Mr Needham, wake up... We've got to get you back to your room so you can go to sleep again. Wake up!

NEEDHAM *(as* PETER *helps him across to the small bedroom)* What're you doing? I don't want to wake up—I'm having a lovely dream. Up, up and away—just want to get my hands on that sporran.

PETER *and* NEEDHAM *go in the small bedroom. The door closes. The study door opens and* SUSAN *and* BARBARA *emerge undressed as before.*

SUSAN We're not waiting any longer. Let's get on with it.

They now see BRIAN *sitting on the sofa stool. They come up to him. He still sits there with his eyes closed.*

Hello, darling. Who are you?

BRIAN *(with eyes closed)* Runnicles.

SUSAN Oh, you're Mr Runnicles, are you?

BRIAN Yes. *(He opens his eyes which are looking down; slowly raising his head; looking a bit higher)* I've never been this close before. *(Pointing at the heather)* What's that?

SUSAN White heather.

BRIAN It's lucky it's there, isn't it? I knew I was going to have a nervous breakdown.

> **BRIAN** *exits to the main bedroom.*

SUSAN That's not what you're having.

> **BARBARA** *and* **SUSAN** *exit after* **BRIAN**.
>
> *The door of the small bedroom opens and* **PETER** *hurries out, looking more worried than ever. He suddenly notices the stool is empty.*

PETER Now, Brian... Good grief! He's gone!

> **PETER** *goes running to the front door and is about to open it when* **BRIAN**'s *voice shrieks out from the main bedroom.*

BRIAN *(offstage)* No, no, I'll catch cold.

> **PETER** *springs to the main bedroom door and opens it. He looks inside, claps his hand over his eyes, and is about to say something when* **BROMHEAD**'s *voice rings out from the stairs.* **PETER** *slams the bedroom door in terror.*
>
> **BROMHEAD** *comes down the stairs preceded by* **FRANCES** *and followed by* **ELEANOR**.

BROMHEAD It really is most kind of you, Eleanor. *(To* **FRANCES***)* And you, too, of course, my dear.

FRANCES *(agitated)* Oh, no, not at all, Mr Bromhead. But, of course, we'd better mention it to Peter first.

ELEANOR I'm sure he'll be only too pleased, Frances. Ah, there you are, Peter. Is anything the matter?

PETER No, no, no—nothing at all. *(He laughs)* I was just going to bring some more coffee up.

BROMHEAD No more for me, thank you, my boy. As a matter of fact, I've started to feel rather tired.

FRANCES Yes, yes, it's surprising how quickly it comes over you, isn't it?

ELEANOR Oh, dear, I've left our bottle of brandy upstairs. I'm sure you'd like a nightcap, wouldn't you, Leslie?

ELEANOR hurries off upstairs.

BROMHEAD Yes, thank you. I don't want to cause an upheaval, Peter. *(He yawns)* Pardon me. But Eleanor here—oh, she's gone—she kindly suggested you might put me up for the night.

PETER What?

FRANCES *(looking at* **PETER***)* I said we'd love to, of course, but Mr Need-ham's in the spare room— *(A thought)* —isn't he?

PETER Yes. Yes, he is, yes.

BROMHEAD No need to go to any trouble. I shall be perfectly happy on the sofa out here.

PETER
FRANCES } No! No! { *(speaking together)*

BROMHEAD No?

PETER No, no, you can't.

FRANCES It's too short for you. I mean you're too tall for it. The couch is far more comfortable.

PETER Yes, yes, far more comfortable.

BROMHEAD *(going to the study)* Thanks very much. You're sure I'm not putting you out, Peter?

PETER Good heavens, no, sir. We couldn't be more delighted.

> **PETER** *gives another false laugh and follows* **BROMHEAD** *into the study.*

> **FRANCES** *turns in despair. She is making for the main bedroom when she is stopped in her tracks by female laughter and a shriek from* **BRIAN** *within.*

SUSAN *(offstage)* Upsidaisy.

BRIAN *(offstage)* Put me down I'm feeling bilious.

> **ELEANOR** *appears on the half-landing.*

ELEANOR Peter is looking after Leslie all right, isn't he, Frances?

FRANCES *(swinging round)* What? Yes, yes, he's making up a bed for him in the other room.

ELEANOR Oh, good. I knew Peter would think of something helpful. *(Giving her the brandy bottle and two glasses)* Leslie's nightcap. Mine is the glass with lipstick on, of course.

FRANCES They've both got lipstick on.

ELEANOR Oh. Well, you'd better give him a clean glass. Shall I bring the coffee things down?

FRANCES No, don't bother. I'll do it. I'm sure you must be feeling tired— *(Hopefully)* —aren't you?

ELEANOR *(going back upstairs)* No, not really. But then I've always been more active at night.

FRANCES *(to herself)* Yes, I'm sure.

> **ELEANOR** *sweeps off with* **FRANCES** *following her. The door of the study opens and* **PETER** *emerges, carrying the girls' two valises with their clothes over his arm.*

PETER Sorry about this jumble, Mr Bromhead. We were sorting a few things out for the Brownies. I'll get you some blankets from the airing cupboard.

> **PETER** *hurries into the bathroom.*

BROMHEAD *(in the doorway)* Very kind of you, my boy. Eleanor was right. I really don't feel up to driving tonight... *(He yawns)*

PETER *(hurrying back to the study with folded blankets)* All right, sir. I'm sure you'll have a good night.

PETER *and* BROMHEAD *exit to the study.*

BRIAN *comes rushing in from the main bedroom on top of* BARBARA. *He is now down to vest, pants and socks.* BARBARA *exits to the bathroom leaving* BRIAN *hanging on a picture like a demented monkey.* SUSAN *follows* BARBARA. PETER *enters from the study and lifts* BRIAN *off the picture.* SUSAN *and* BARBARA *return from the bathroom.*

SUSAN Mr Runnicles.

In his blind panic, BRIAN *dives headfirst through the hatch into the kitchen. The hatch crashes down.* BRIAN *totters out of the kitchen with his head through the vegetable picture and, in his bemused state, goes straight out through the front door.*

PETER What in God's name are you doing now? Don't you people ever take no for an answer? Can't you understand: we don't want you here—any of us. We just want you to put your clothes on and go—leave—get out.

SUSAN Do you mean you've had enough?

PETER More than enough. We didn't want anything to start with.

SUSAN You didn't? Well, there must be something wrong with all of you, then. You can't be normal.

PETER Would you please get dressed and go!

SUSAN Yes! O.K. *(She starts for the study)*

PETER Thank God for that! *(He suddenly realizes they are making for* BROMHEAD's *room)* No, no, not in there! They're in the bathroom—in the bathroom!

SUSAN There's no need to shout, Mr Hunter. We may have lost everything else, but we still have our dignity.

PETER *is taken aback. He turns and goes towards the kitchen, shouting.*

PETER Brian! Brian!

Now the door of the small bedroom opens and a semi-sensible NEEDHAM *stands there, wrapped in an eiderdown.*

NEEDHAM Excuse me—is that—Mr Bromhead at last?

FRANCES *appears at the top of the stairs.*

PETER Beg pardon? No—no, it's—it's— *(He sees* FRANCES *coming downstairs with trays and cups)* —it's my wife coming downstairs, that's all.

NEEDHAM How long have I been asleep, Mr Hunter?

PETER Ages. Mr Bromhead's retired now.

NEEDHAM *(befuddled)* Has he, really? At his age? What a pity.

FRANCES *puts the tray on the counter.*

FRANCES Is anything the matter, Mr Needham?

NEEDHAM Must've been my sleeping capsule—had a very odd effect—most disturbing.

FRANCES Oh, dear.

NEEDHAM Yes, I think I'd better have another one.

FRANCES Would you like me to get it for you? *(She goes to the kitchen)*

NEEDHAM Yes, please. *(As* FRANCES *goes into the kitchen)* I think it might be better if I postponed my—inspection for a bit, Mr Hunter.

PETER Postpone it? You're not feeling ill, are you, Mr Needham?

NEEDHAM No, no, not at all. It's just that I've been away from home for rather a long time and there are one or two things I want to go through with my wife.

FRANCES *(coming back with a glass of sleeping draught)* Here you are, Mr Needham. You'll soon be asleep again.

NEEDHAM Yes, yes, I do hope I will. *(He downs the draught in one)* I'm really looking forward to it. Good night, Mrs and Mr Hunter.

PETER Happy dreams.

NEEDHAM Yes, very, thank you.

> **NEEDHAM** *goes back to his room. As he closes his door,* **SUSAN** *and* **BARBARA** *enter from the bathroom, fully dressed and carrying their cases.*

SUSAN Right. That's it. We're packed and we're off. And we're sorry we're not what you needed. *(Seeing* **FRANCES***)* Hello, who are you?

FRANCES I'm Frances Hunter.

SUSAN Oh, we know who he is. And you're newly married. Now we know why he doesn't need us. Can we get a cab anywhere?

PETER Never mind a cab. Can you drive?

SUSAN I can't but she can. *(Indicating* **BARBARA***)* Barbara's got a licence for everything.

PETER *(giving* **BARBARA** *the ignition keys and the last of the books)* Here you are then. There's a van downstairs full of books. You can take them to your Mr Nikolaides and tell him we don't want them—or anything else at all. Oh, and you can leave the van at any of their depots, and there's a few more books in the bedroom we don't want.

SUSAN *(to* **BARBARA***)* Oh, well. We're getting an early night for a change. That's something, I suppose.

FRANCES *(taking* **PETER***'s arm)* You won't send us anything else now, will you? We're really very happy as we are.

SUSAN I'm sure you are.

FRANCES And you'd better tell Mr Nicolathingummy to change his advert. He might get some more like us by mistake.

SUSAN Mistake? It isn't a mistake. He does it on purpose, love— to expand the market. And do you know something—you're the first to complain. And you stay like that. Good luck.

PETER } Good night. Keep your licence clean, Barbara.

FRANCES } Good-bye.

    SUSAN *and* BARBARA *exit, closing the front door.*

    PETER *and* FRANCES *collapse into each other's arms on the sofa stool.*

PETER My God, what an experience, I'd never have dreamed it possible.

FRANCES There must be a lot of very odd people about.

PETER Yes, there must be—anyway, we're on our own again at last.

    ELEANOR *appears on the landing.*

ELEANOR Are you there, Peter?

PETER Oh, God! Yes, what is it?

ELEANOR Did I leave my chocolates down here? Oh, yes. *(She picks them up)* I do so enjoy a little nibble in bed. Good night, darlings.

FRANCES Good night.

ELEANOR *(pausing again)* Oh, how silly of me. I haven't told you my wonderful news, have I?

FRANCES Your wonderful news?

ELEANOR Yes, I'm not going to my health farm after all.

PETER You aren't?

ELEANOR No, I've persuaded Leslie to take a holiday so I've invited him to stay.

PETER Stay?

FRANCES Here?

ELEANOR No, no, my dears, of course not—with me in Chelsea. We're going to have a week of culture—the National Gallery, the National Theatre and Darling Danny-La-Rue. We're leaving tomorrow. It'll be such fun. Good night.

ELEANOR goes upstairs again.

FRANCES throws her arms round PETER's neck.

FRANCES It's too good to be true. They're leaving tomorrow, darling.

PETER I know, I know.

There is a knock at the front door. PETER groans and automatically goes and opens it.

Superintendent PAUL enters carrying the semi-sensible BRIAN in his arms.

PAUL Sorry to disturb you, Mr Hunter, but I've just found Mr Runnicles like this asleep on a dustbin.

FRANCES On a dustbin?

PAUL Yes, and the side door was wide open again, of course.

PETER I'm terribly sorry, Superintendent: he's supposed to be spending the night here.

FRANCES Yes, I expect he's been sleep-walking again. He's had rather a tiring day.

BRIAN *(stirring)* I want to confess—but it wasn't only me—it was...

PETER Yes, yes, yes, Brian. Never mind all that. Let's lie him down here, Superintendent.

FRANCES I'll get a blanket.

FRANCES *exits to the bathroom.*

PETER *(as they lie* BRIAN *down on the studio couch)* He often has nightmares like this. It's nothing unusual.

PAUL He's been rambling like this ever since I found him—a lot of gibberish about a mauve vegetable painter, a parrot, and white heather on his honorarium.

PETER Oh, his honorarium—that sounds like his Round Table charity committee.

PAUL Oh, yes—our sports and social club are making a contribution. We're giving them the proceeds from our next stag night.

PETER Stag night?

PAUL Yes, you must come along—next Friday. One of your inspectors is coming—what's his name? —Needham.

PETER Mr Arnold Needham?

PAUL That's it. Great friend of the Assistant Commissioner. *(He nudges* PETER *slyly)* We're showing all those films from St Mark's Bazaar.

PETER I don't believe it.

PAUL You will when you see them—especially Dick Turpin rides again and again and again. *(He laughs)* Good night, Mrs Hunter.

As PAUL *makes for the front door,* FRANCES *comes out of the bathroom carrying some blankets and a pillow.*

FRANCES Good night, Superintendent.

PAUL *exits briskly.*

(to PETER*)* Is everything still all right, darling?

PETER All right? You've no idea, darling—they're all at it.

BRIAN *(stirring)* Yes, they're all at it—everyone on the Table a bumper effort—but I'm too tired to go.

PETER Yes, I'm sure you are, Brian. Just go to sleep.

FRANCES What on earth is he moaning about now?

PETER I don't know—and I don't care. Come on—we're going to bed.

FRANCES What about the washing up?

PETER To hell with the washing up, let's just go to bed—our bed, darling.

FRANCES Yes, darling.

FRANCES *and* PETER *are just going into the main bedroom when there is a loud knocking at the front door.*

Oh, no, not again. *(Pleading)* Don't answer it, Peter. Please don't answer it.

PETER No. I'm not going to, darling—not for anybody, I promise. That door is not going to open again tonight.

The knocking continues.

The study door opens and BROMHEAD *comes out in shirt and trousers.*

BROMHEAD *(brusquely)* Peter, aren't you going to open the door? We'll never get any sleep with all that infernal knocking going on.

PETER Open the door, sir. Oh, yes—yes, yes, of course, sir.

More knocking at the door.

BROMHEAD Well, go on, man, do it. It'll wake Eleanor up.

PETER Yes, sir—all right, sir...

PETER *opens the front door, to reveal* SUSAN *and* BARBARA *standing outside, then very quickly shuts it again all but a foot.*

BROMHEAD *turns to go back to his room.*

SUSAN *(off; very loudly)* Sorry, but we had to come back. We forgot about the cheque.

BROMHEAD *hears the word "cheque" and turns in his tracks.* FRANCES *senses all is up.*

PETER *(hissing)* Never mind about that now.

BROMHEAD Cheque? What cheque?

SUSAN *(offstage)* The guv'nor says can he have cash to help with his surtax— 'stead of this cheque from Jordan Electrics.

BROMHEAD Jordan Electrics? That's one of my accounts.

BRIAN *(comatose)* Pretty Polly. Pretty Polly.

BROMHEAD Quiet, Runnicles. What the devil's going on here? Let the young lady in at once, Peter.

PETER *(turning away in despair)* That's it then—it's all over now—all over.

SUSAN *and* BARBARA *enter the room.*

FRANCES *(going to him)* Darling, I'm so sorry—so sorry. It was all my fault, Mr Bromhead.

ELEANOR *appears on the stairs.*

ELEANOR What on earth is going on down here? I thought we were all in bed. And who are these two young women?

BROMHEAD Two young women? I haven't the least idea. *(He turns to face the girls for the first time)* Oh, good grief.

SUSAN *(recognizing him instantly)* Hello. Fancy meeting you here, love. Look, Barbara, it's our Mr Smith. We haven't seen you for weeks, and you used to be so regular. We're taking Barclaycards now, you know.

BROMHEAD Oh, dear. Oh, dear.

FRANCES Mr Bromhead, really. } *(speaking together)*

PETER Mr Bromhead.

The door of the small bedroom opens and **NEEDHAM** *stands there in his pyjamas.*

NEEDHAM Is that Mr Bromhead at last?

BRIAN Yes, that's Mr Bromhead. I know Mr Bromhead very well.

There is a general commotion which is soon silenced by three loud knocks at the front door.

PETER What have they sent us now?

PETER *opens the door to Superintendent* **PAUL**, *who is carrying a box.*

PAUL Ah, Mr Hunter, I've found a man downstairs with a parcel.

PETER Whatever it is I don't want it.

PAUL Oh, it's not for you, sir. It's addressed to Mr Runnicles.

BRIAN *looks at the parcel and at Superintendent* **PAUL** *who is coming towards him. It is all too much for him, he throws the blanket over his head and with shouts of "No, no, no, no", he dives through the closed hatch, as—the curtain falls.*

FURNITURE AND PROPERTY LIST

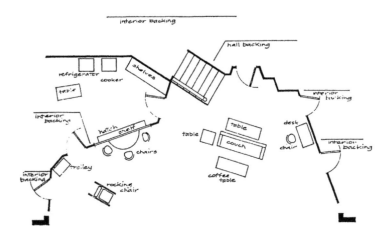

ACT I, SCENE ONE

On stage: Living-Room:

Desk. *On it:* lamp, writing materials, notepaper, envelopes. *In drawer:* Sellotape, cheque-book. *Under it:* metal waste bin with smoke effect and blackened flower

Drinks trolley. *On it:* brandy, whisky, gin, Dubonnet, lemon and squeezer, empty soda syphon, glasses. *On lower shelf:* TV set

Sofa table. *On it:* briefcase

Coffee-table

Small occasional table to side of couch. *On it:* lamp, large table lighter

Studio couch

Rocking chair

3 small chairs below hatch shelf

On wall near front door: wall speakers to bank and to outer door

On wall over bathroom door: picture securely fastened to bear Brian's weight

Floor and stair carpets

Kitchen:
Double sink with waste disposal unit
Cupboards. *In them:* crockery, glasses, tin of biscuits,
    bottle of vodka, electric light bulb, tea, coffee
Electric cooker
Refrigerator. *In it:* milk
Table. *On it:* 2 mugs of coffee, tray, plate of toast,
    flower vase. *In drawers:* cutlery
On draining-board: crockery, cloths

Offstage: Small valise (**ELEANOR**)
           2 bouquets of flowers (**ELEANOR**)
           2 suitcases, one very large (**ELEANOR**)
           Sheaf of papers and cheques (**PETER**)
           Still life painting, wrapped (**BRIAN**)
           Electric blanket, transistor radio, Teasmaid (**PETER**)
           Large brown-paper-wrapped box, sealed with wax,
               with detachable label, containing envelopes of
               dirty photographs (**BRIAN**)
           Garden trowel (**BRIAN**)
           Washbag (**BRIAN**)

Personal: **Peter:** keys, tiepin
           Brian: Scout knife

SCENE TWO

Strike: Flower stalks
           Contents of waste bin
           Vase

Set: Plate of cocktail snacks and bowl of cheese dip on
               kitchen table
           Plate of sandwiches on kitchen table
           Waste bin under desk
           A–Z of London on desk
           Ice bucket by refrigerator
           Vase in kitchen
           Tidy room generally

Offstage: Bouquet of flowers (**ELEANOR**)

Local newspaper (**ELEANOR**)
Local newspaper (**BRIAN**)
Wrapped box containing rolls of film and note
   (**Brian**)
Still life from Scene One (**ELEANOR**)
Clipboard, pencil, envelope with invoice (**DELIVERY
   MAN**)
Trolley with 2 enormous cartons (**DELIVERY MAN**)

ACT II

Strike: Cartons and lorry
            All remaining dirty glasses and dishes
            Newspapers

Set: Tidy room generally

Offstage: Several piles of large uniformly plastic-bound books
                 (**PETER, FRANCES, BRIAN**)
            Cup and saucer (**ELEANOR**)
            Emery boards (**FRANCES**)
            Heart-shaped box of chocolates (**BROMHEAD**)
            Overnight case (**NEEDHAM**)
            Spongebag (**NEEDHAM**)
            Bottle of capsules (**NEEDHAM**)
            Valise (**SUSAN**)
            Valise (**BARBARA**)
            Rubber club ((**SUSAN**)
            Plastic thistle (**BARBARA**)
            Blankets (**PETER**)
            Blankets and pillow (**FRANCES**)
            Large paper-wrapped box (**PAUL**)

Personal: **PETER:** invoice, ignition keys
            NEEDHAM: row of pens

LIGHTING PLOT

Property fittings required: wall-brackets, table lamps
A living-room and kitchen. The same scene throughout

ACT I, SCENE ONE

Morning

To open:	General effect of bright daylight
Cue 1	**ELEANOR :** "My flowers!" (Page 36)
	Blackout.

ACT I, SCENE TWO

Early evening

To open:	General effect of summer evening daylight
	No cues.

ACT II

Evening

To open:	All interior lighting full up
	No cues.

EFFECTS PLOT

ACT I SCENE ONE

Cue 1	**FRANCES:** "...see that you do."	(Page 5)
	Bank buzzer sounds.	
Cue 2	**PETER:** "...you do exaggerate..."	(Page 8)
	Bank buzzer sounds three times.	
Cue 3	**FRANCES** goes to the bathroom	(Page 8)
	Bath water effect, followed by door buzzer.	

TV Newscaster off.

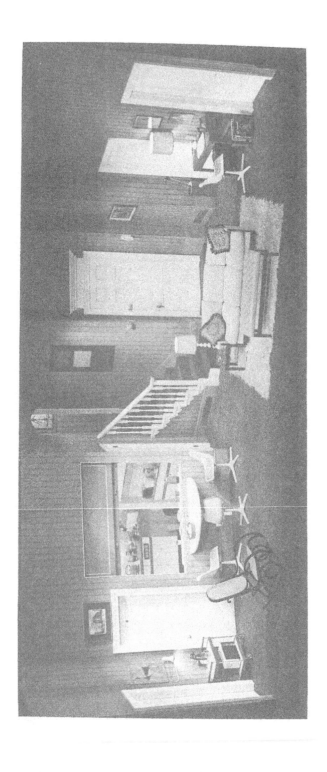

VISIT THE
SAMUEL FRENCH
BOOKSHOP
AT THE
ROYAL COURT THEATRE

Browse plays and theatre books,
get expert advice and enjoy a coffee

Samuel French Bookshop
Royal Court Theatre
Sloane Square
London
SW1W 8AS
020 7565 5024

Shop from thousands of titles
on our website

 samuelfrench.co.uk

 samuelfrenchltd

 samuel french uk

Lightning Source UK Ltd.
Milton Keynes UK
UKHW021321240322
400559UK00011B/60